THE
Afterlife
HEALING
CIRCLE

THE
Afterlife
HEALING
CIRCLE

How Anyone Can Contact
the Other Side

Candace L. Talmadge
and Jana L. Simons

Foreword by Raymond Moody, MD

New Page Books
A division of The Career Press, Inc.
Pompton Plains, N.J.

THE AFTERLIFE HEALING CIRCLE
EDITED AND TYPESET BY KARA KUMPEL
Cover design by Howard Grossman/12E Design
Printed in the U.S.A.

To order this title, please call toll-free 1-800-CAREER-1 (NJ and Canada: 201-848-0310) to order using VISA or MasterCard, or for further information on books from Career Press.

The Career Press, Inc.
220 West Parkway, Unit 12
Pompton Plains, NJ 07444
www.careerpress.com
www.newpagebooks.com

Library of Congress Cataloging-in-Publication Data
Talmadge, Candace L., 1954- author.
 The afterlife healing circle : how anyone can contact the other side / by Candace L. Talmadge and Jana L. Simons ; foreword by Raymond Moody, MD.
    pages cm
 Includes bibliographical references and index.
  ISBN 978-1-60163-373-6 (paperback) -- ISBN 978-1-60163-379-8 (ebook) 1. Seances. 2. Spiritualism. I. Simons, Jana L., 1945- author. II. Moody, Raymond A., writer of foreword. III. Title.
  BF1261.2.T35 2015
  133.9'1--dc23
                                                    2015002857

This book is dedicated to all of the souls who reach across dimensions to connect with those they love.

Acknowledgments

Many have offered support and assistance to help this book reach publication. We want to acknowledge our two soul-sisters. One is Pam Worthington-Lash, who read the manuscript numerous times and asked excellent questions that prompted us to keep improving it. The other is Susanne Thibodeau, who provided insights and extensive moral support along the way.

We acknowledge the significant contributions of clients and students who either requested the afterlife healing circle or sat in on one and then shared their stories in these pages. Thank you. We also thank those who told us their stories of communicating with the other side and allowed us to include them in this book. Such deeply personal sharing takes courage and generosity.

We are grateful to our agent, John White, for his tireless efforts on our behalf, and to Raymond Moody, MD, who told us about John and then crafted a lyrical Foreword for this book. To know that our work touched one of the pioneers of the afterlife movement means a great deal to us.

Fellow author Mark Ireland deserves our thanks for his efforts to support us, too. He helped bring about a vastly improved manuscript that is the basis for this book. We also wish to thank Terri Daniel for making sure we connected with Dr. Moody.

We want to acknowledge and thank our unseen mentors and colleagues of the Sunan Society and our own groups of spirit guides. They are indeed part of that wider community we define and discuss in this book and have been with us every step of the way, even throughout many years of discouragement. They never gave up on us, and that helped us keep going. This book is one of the fruits of our collaboration.

Contents

Foreword

by Raymond Moody, MD

All over the world, and from prehistoric times, human beings have attempted to contact the spirits of their loved ones lost to death. Modern mediumship, we are told, dates from the 19th century, but that is a mere factoid or a kind of urban myth. In reality, for more than ten thousand years, people have known of various methods for carrying on active relationships with their deceased relatives. A loving relationship with a person doesn't stop when that individual dies, and that has been true throughout human history.

The Afterlife Healing Circle describes an exciting re-discovery and updating of ancient shamanic modalities for communicating with the spirit world and making it manifest in the physical world. The book is replete with fascinating case histories and personal experiential accounts of life-changing spiritual encounters. Reading *The Afterlife Healing Circle* reminded me again of a remarkable cultural and historical fact about spiritual experiences: People living in advanced Western societies frequently have profound episodes of spiritual consciousness. Similar episodes are well-known, named, and categorized in various non-Western lands and tribal societies, yet knowledge of such kinds of experiences is not culturally transmitted in the Western world. In other words, certain kinds of spiritual experiential formats or potentialities are somehow built into the human mind. And such experiences will occur to people regardless of whether that particular kind of experience is acknowledged and catalogued in those people's cultural traditions or not.

For instance, in China, there is an ancient, well-established tradition of what are known as birth dreams. Pregnant Chinese mothers often communicate through dreams with the yet-to-be-born individuals they are carrying in their wombs. In China, this is all acknowledged, understood, and appreciated. Yet the same thing happens among Americans as well, as a poignant story in this book illustrates, despite the cultural void that surrounds the phenomenon in the United States.

To me, this is an astonishing fact about human nature. There is a universal format, as it were, of spiritual experiences deeply embedded in us all that transcends particular human cultures. *The Afterlife Healing Circle* touches on this and many other important, unexplored domains of human consciousness. As this book shows, unleashing such hidden spiritual powers can greatly benefit the living and perhaps bring balance to the dead.

Raymond Moody, MD, is a psychiatrist and author of the international bestselling book Life After Life *about the near-death experience, a term he coined. His pioneering research into the question of life after death helped legitimize the subject. In the 1970s he and a small group of fellow researchers formed the International Association for Near-Death Studies (IANDS), which continues today as one aspect of the worldwide study of the case for postmortem existence.*

Introduction

What kind of world would we inhabit if we were not so terrified of death? If we could meet our children and know their lives' purposes and at least some of their emotional and spiritual needs before they were born? Imagine greater freedom from fear. Imagine parents being better prepared and wiser stewards of young lives.

If the preceding seems unobtainable, please read this book. It *is* possible because it *has* happened. We, the authors of this book, have witnessed the afterlife healing circle alleviating decades of unresolved grief. We also have firsthand knowledge of the way the afterlife healing circle can ease the fears of expectant parents. This book recounts some of the stories of those involved.

There is no greater joy than to help someone move from pain and despair to hope and resolution. It has been our privilege throughout many years to assist in making this happen, and we wrote this book to help anyone who desires to do the same.

Most books about the afterlife fall into one of several groupings. Some recount scientific research into the survival of consciousness after the physical body's death, while others relate the personal near-death experiences of credentialed experts. Other such books reveal how an ordinary person or child died, glimpsed the other side, and returned to tell about it. The fourth type of afterlife tome is written by mediums or psychics who discuss their experiences contacting souls on behalf of their clients.

This book does not fall into any of these categories. Instead, it is a how-to manual with enough context to explain the why-to, when-to, and where-to. You need not be an expert or medium, or even think of yourself as specially gifted in any way, to conduct or participate in the afterlife healing circle. The desire to help someone else or to heal your own pain, along with some practice in the intuition-tapping approaches we provide in this book, go a long way.

You do not make this journey alone. The afterlife healing circle brings together informal groups of family, friends, and neighbors who assist and support those in need of healing. Filled with tears, laughter, and, frequently, surprises, the afterlife healing circle is one of the most profound spiritual gifts we can give each other, and ourselves. The true impact of the afterlife healing circle is the *experience* of the other side that it provides to participants. That distinguishes it from a reading by a medium or from books about scientific experiments concerning the afterlife. What also sets it apart is its use for contacting souls *before* the birth of the physical body, not just after its demise. It's possible to contact souls regardless of whether or not they inhabit bodies we perceive as physical. We do this often in our work as Sunan therapists.

The afterlife healing circle is a grassroots spiritual practice with enormous potential to bring about inner peace. The simple method outlined in these pages equips ordinary people to find their own answers to life's deepest questions without relying on authorities or experts.

That in itself is a world-changing proposition.

Ours is not an organized movement with an agenda or over-arching goals. Instead, we hope that by publishing a book that teaches anyone how to conduct the afterlife healing circle, we will help foster a jubilant inner shift in awareness as more of us experience and embrace the reality of love and consciousness as a continuum, whether expressed in this world or any other.

Chapter 1

Ever watch *The Changling*? There's a corker of a scene in this movie. A medium ostensibly in a trance state supposedly does automatic writing. Thunder booms; the wind howls; the shutters bang open and shut; the lights flicker on and off; a huge chandelier swings ominously above the woman and other participants in the event. It's meant to be dramatic, but the effect is laughable. It's just a lot of hoopla and weird goings-on. Right now readers may be wondering, *What does this scene have to do with the afterlife healing circle? It's about a séance!*

Our answer is nothing—and yet a lot. The big-screen drama has precious little to do with what actually happens during the afterlife healing circle as we practice it, or with any of the legitimate reasons for conducting one in the first place. But whether we like it or not, our use of the afterlife healing circle has been known more commonly as the séance, even if the two are as different as day and night.

We wrote this book to explain how and why our version of the afterlife healing circle is a powerful grassroots spiritual tool and nothing at all like the séance, its much-better-known step-sibling. In the next chapter we will look briefly at how the circle has been associated with healing and the sacred, from ancient times to the present and in multiple societies across the world. We are not new in using the circle as a healing tool, but we are advocating an approach that brings all of self to the circle and thus makes a type of communication possible in ways not generally associated with the more prevalent uses of the healing circle.

To succeed, we must shatter the séance stereotype that was born out of ignorance and prejudice against the emotional and spiritual (intuitive) parts of self. Derided by some, proscribed by others, the séance is, tragically, degenerate fodder for side shows. One such spectacle was witnessed in Las Vegas a number of years ago by paranormal author and lecturer Ken Hudnall. Ken, a prolific author who hosts an online radio program called *The Ken Hudnall Show*, was in Sin City doing a ghost tour that ended with a séance. He was suspicious from the outset because he was not allowed to inspect the room prior to the event. To up the drama factor, the stagers included elements of Voodoo and Santeria among the séance rituals with which Ken is very familiar. There were chicken bones in motion, a tambourine playing, and objects on the table that appeared to be moving by themselves.

"It's easy to spot collusion," Ken says, "because usually somebody in the audience is a shill." But on this occasion, he could not figure it out, and remains puzzled to this day.

"At the end of the séance," he explains, "the lights go out, the medium begins to scream, there's a big bang, and the girl beside me jumps into my lap," Ken recalls. "When the lights come on, I'm holding the girl and the medium has vanished. Everybody was absolutely fascinated, and I'm looking for the trick."

Trickery and the séance have gone hand in hand too often, such as a séance in Grosse Point Farms, Michigan, in the 1940s that was intended to be sham. Two college students who were amateur magicians and known locally as séance debunkers received $100 to stage a fake séance in an affluent woman's home. On the appointed night, the event appeared to go off without a hitch. There were eerie sounds, and a likeness of the dead husband of one of the guests appeared out of a mist to answer her questions.

Afterward, the student who led the séance wandered into the kitchen and found his partner pounding on the back door. This second student, who was to work the apparatus to generate the special effects, had been locked outside throughout the entire evening and had been unable to play his backstage role.[1]

Unnerving, isn't it? Especially for those who are convinced the whole séance proposition (and, by extension, the afterlife healing circle) is always phony.

Those students' experience in the bizarre has been shared by countless others. People often dabble in the séance as a casual pastime with no more apparent significance or meaning than a game. It begins as a lark or a joke to alleviate boredom, to enliven a party gone flat, or to satisfy idle curiosity by seeing if something or someone really is "out there." This casual approach is begging for problems if not downright disaster. Unaware of what they're really getting into, many people make well-meaning attempts at spirit communication. They try table tipping or Ouija boards, which may be sold as games but are not toys. A young woman we'll call Tammy Jenkins found this out the hard way.

Scared and bewildered, Tammy, who declined to provide her full name, phoned us one day, desperate for reassurance. She also wanted an explanation for the chilling and bizarre event she had just experienced. She and a friend had decided to use a Ouija board to contact her late grandfather. Things went fine at first. The pointer, moving under their hands, spelled out the nickname her grandfather had always called her.

Then it stopped. Something changed. The pointer moved again but haphazardly, as though whoever or whatever was propelling it didn't recognize Tammy or her friend. It tried to spell out a word that appeared to be "help," then spun around and around in wild circles. At that instant both young women experienced a nasty feeling in their stomachs. Their eyes blurred, and Tammy recalled actually dozing off for a brief period. After they ended the session, all the tapes on top of the VCR fell sideways and spilled onto the floor. No one was anywhere close to the tapes when they fell.

Tammy's unnerving tale of her experiences with a Ouija board incidents is by no means unusual. A visitor on the Yahoo.com Answers Website tells about dabbling with a Ouija board at a slumber party in the sixth grade. Immediately after the kids asked about the entity that responded to their summons, all of the faucets in the bathroom turned on. No one could have entered the bathroom without being noticed because it opened only to the bedroom. "It was pretty scary," the poster writes.[2]

The séance is probably the most misunderstood and thus abused and debased of all spiritual practices. The very word immediately brings to mind what most of us consider the unreal and therefore absurd notion of "conjuring up spirits." The séance stereotype certainly was the foundation for that outrageous scene in *The Changling,* and a much more recent séance-related movie even has that word in the title: *The Conjuring.* Skeptics' view of the séance can be summed up by Brian Dunning, who writes the Skeptoid blog: "Contacting the dead has never passed any kind of controlled test, has no plausible theory, and is a fraud committed upon susceptible consumers," he asserts.[3]

Members of some religious communities share the same attitude, although for different reasons. Texas resident Jeanne M. Perdue cited Ecclesiastes 9:5–6 in the Bible as her caution against contacting the dead: "For the living know that they will die, but the dead know nothing at all, nor do they have any more reward, because all memory of them is forgotten. Also, their love and their hate and their jealousy have already perished, and they no longer have any share in what is done under the sun."

The S-word also evokes a good deal of fear. "Trying to contact the departed through Ouija boards, séances, etc., is one of the most dangerous things anyone can do," warns Phyllis Sloan, PhD, an author and spiritual science minister based in Maryland. "It is playing Russian roulette trying to contact spirits. God does not like it and the punishment is severe."[4]

We all have our own understanding about what God does or does not like or allow. And we, the authors, would argue that negative events are more about experiencing the consequences of our beliefs and actions than about divine punishment. We agree, however, that there certainly has been a great deal of fraud involving séances in recent decades, if not centuries. We also are well-aware of the potential for hazards. The good news is these dangers can be avoided, and one reason this book exists is to teach readers how to do just that.

Here's the bottom line: The afterlife healing circle is simply one means by which those in physical bodies may communicate with those who are not—meaning those who are on the other side. It makes no difference whether those who do not have physical bodies are considered dead or not yet born. We use what we call the afterlife healing circle to experience the reality of being (life) as a continuum—after physical death and before physical birth.

Personal experience then enables us to decide for ourselves, rather than take someone else's word for it, what we believe about the possibility of multiple lives and what transpires before birth and after death. We need to experience this for ourselves because that is the most engaging and compelling way we learn and grow. A Chinese proverb sums this up best. It states, "Tell me and I'll forget. Show me and I may remember. Involve me and I will understand." Only direct personal experience enables us to even begin to comprehend a subject that seems at first unfathomable or bizarre.

Conducted correctly, our version of the afterlife healing circle is one of the most powerful spiritual and emotional experiences available to anyone in a group setting. Moreover, learning to conduct the afterlife healing circle and participating in it is grassroots spirituality at its purest, under the direction of those involved, acting as their own connections to spirit and not relying on intermediaries' interpretations or dogmas. Knowing for ourselves more about what happens after the physical body dies, or before it is born, is empowering and freeing in ways too numerous to count or even understand without having had the actual experience.

So, if conducting a séance can and does lead to trouble, why do it at all, even under a different label? That's a valid and pertinent question. Indeed, Phyllis Sloane, the minister and author who states she is also a psychic and clairvoyant, advises that the best route is simply to pray for information from God about those not in physical bodies. "Spirits at this plane are evil," she says, "and they impersonate those who may be heroes of those who hear them. I have been in this field as well as psychotherapy for over 40 years and I cannot tell you how many people have run into serious trouble with contacting spirits. Some have never recovered. They become what medicine calls schizophrenic."[5]

We respect her concerns because they are valid. We certainly agree that prayer is beneficial, which is why we do it daily in our own ways. But we have been conducting and taking part in our version of the afterlife healing circle for decades with no adverse effects for ourselves or those who also participate. The properly conducted afterlife healing circle involves no danger, as this book will explain and demonstrate.

Moreover, we often need resolution that we cannot find or obtain through more conventional means, such as prayer, meditation, or counseling. In Chapter 3, we will introduce you to a woman we refer to as Clara Jones to maintain her privacy. For 20 years she tried both psychiatry and psychotherapy. They were very helpful for her but, in the end, both were simply too limited in approach or understanding to address the one issue that was still eating away at her. After all of her treatment and hard work on self, she still yearned for emotional and spiritual resolution with her dead mother.

This longing is universal. Astrid Stromberg, PhD, says callers to her *Brilliant Essence* radio show who mention departed loved ones invariably have unresolved issues concerning their deaths. "Usually people start out by saying, 'Are they okay?'" explains Stromberg, an inspirational speaker. "But what they really want to say is, 'Do they still feel my love? Do they still feel the connection? Do they still see me live? Do they still know how I feel? Do they know how their experience of them dying was felt by me and the ones who lost them?'"[6]

In other words, when someone we love and care about dies, we experience a profound and painful disconnection and loss, and we cannot help but long to reverse it or at least alleviate it. The problem, for Clara and many others, is that traditional psychotherapy provides little to no help in relieving grief, and unresolved grief can cause significant mental and emotional distress.[7]

A similar emotional and spiritual crisis can result from an unwanted or poorly timed pregnancy. That was the issue of another woman we will tell you about named Debra Wilde (a pseudonym to protect her privacy). She needed emotional and spiritual support to resolve her fear and self-doubt. Parents-to-be Marc and Rondi H. (their last name abbreviated for privacy) also required something that no doctor or pregnancy counselor, however expert and well-intentioned, could give them. They needed to *feel* reassured and confident in their hearts and souls, not just know in their heads, that the pregnancy and birth were going to be fine.

Part of the issue is simply that traditional psycho-therapy, grounded in behavioral and cognitive sciences, is too limited to admit the possibility of life beyond the physical, whether it's after death or before birth. Science speaks to and satisfies the mental part of our being, but offers nothing to fill or even acknowledge the very different needs of the emotional and spiritual parts of self. This half of self knows and senses that the physical is not the only reality, and its legitimate needs deserve as much respect and support as the mental part's interest in science.

The afterlife healing circle speaks to all of self, not just one or two parts. Briana Henderson Saussy is an intuitive counselor and teacher who helps clients access their ancestors and ancestral knowing. Very familiar with circles, she says, "A circle gives you a safe place where you can feel your pain, you can feel your disori-entation, you can feel your grief, and it's grounded and protected so you can feel these things and not be de-voured by them, not be incapacitated by them."[8]

Precisely. Within the circle it is safe to vent one's grief and anguish, surrounded by loving support. But beyond providing a safe place in which to express pain, the circle as we practice it can help launch or accelerate healing, too. Healing, which we will define in greater detail in Chapter 2, is the purpose of the circle. It heals, in part, by providing uniquely personal answers to those questions that Astrid outlines. This approach also heals by respecting and then restoring or establishing an emotional and spiritual connection to the beloved departed or the not yet born.

The afterlife healing circle cannot, however, substitute for a deeper exploration of unresolved matters between the living and souls on the other side (the dead and the not yet born). This is one of the afterlife healing circle's limitations. It is not the same as therapy, and therefore is not an appropriate place to explore very sensitive issues, such as sexual abuse, that are best addressed in a private setting with either a traditional or alternative therapist or counselor. Nor can the afterlife healing circle function as an experiment or provide objective proof of anything. It offers only an entirely subjective experience and should be employed and regarded as such. There is nothing dangerous or negative about subjectivity, provided we do not insist that our subjective experiences determine the reality or lives of others.

The power of the afterlife healing circle is directly related to the presence of love, the most subjective factor of all. Love helps heal a lot of the pain caused by the separation that we call death, and eases the soul's entry into the physical body that we refer to as birth.

The desire for resolution is sometimes so strong that, if unfulfilled, it can lead to serious consequences. One such consequence is poltergeist phenomena. A poltergeist is thought to be present when objects, some of which can be alarmingly big and heavy, move, fall, and even become airborne of their own volition. Parapsychologists and other researchers have conducted extensive studies of poltergeist events. They have found one element common to the majority of these instances: the presence of a female, usually a girl in her pre-teens or teens, or sometimes a young woman in her 20s. Researchers have noted the female's presence without any true understanding of its connection to the phenomena of self-propelled objects.

We believe the poltergeist is misunderstood. In our opinion, a poltergeist is most often not a separate soul or entity tossing objects about at random. Rather, the poltergeist effect is rooted in the suppression and denial of anger, one of the strongest of all emotions. And what has always been the most unacceptable emotion for a girl or woman to display in societies all around the globe? Anger, of course.

From our work in alternative therapy, we know that we store anger in the subconscious mind, also known as the emotional body. We offer the following as an alternative explanation for poltergeist phenomena: When a girl's or woman's anger, suppressed and denied in this lifetime and in many past lives, reaches a certain intensity, it can no longer be contained within the person's own subconscious. It then explodes outward with enough force to move even huge physical objects. Rage expressed in such a manner would most certainly appear random or chaotic to the conscious mind. That's because the expression is at the emotional, non-rational level. The female involved is unaware of her participation in creating the phenomena. Such females are consistently observed to be subdued, obedient "good girls."

They have been figuratively swallowing their rage for a long time.

The poltergeist effect, then, is an extreme and frightening form of passive-aggressive behavior. It is an unavoidable signal from the emotional body that this person, at least on some deeper level, wants her rage and pain to be acknowledged and healed. It is far beyond the scope of the afterlife healing circle, however, to offer the depth and extent of healing needed in cases of poltergeist phenomena. These women very much need something effective in addressing their wounded emotional bodies.

Far more terrifying than poltergeist phenomena are those documented cases of possession. This phenomenon is so baffling that science cannot explain it and therefore tends to dismiss it. The Church explains possession as the means by which the devil or his minions corrupt good people and turn them against God.

We have our own theories about possession. We are skeptical of the terms *diabolic* and *demonic*. We do agree that something or someone invades the physical body of an incarnated soul, but rather than being satanic, that something is what we would call a *denial spirit*. A denial spirit denies Creation and God's light and unconditional love. Explaining how denial spirits originally came to be within Creation is way beyond the scope of this book. Those interested in this topic may want to read the series of books by Ceanne de Rohan.[9]

It's enough to say that denial spirits exist, even if the rational part of the mind finds them and the havoc and devastation they wreak too incredible to acknowl-edge without firsthand experience—and sometimes even with that experience. Denial spirits are not en-lightened or loving, obviously. Given half a chance, a denial spirit will invade a physical body that does not belong to it as a way to deny the existence of the soul to which that physical vehicle does belong. Denial spir-its get that opportunity when we open ourselves up to the universe without realizing the full implications of what we are doing or without knowing how to protect ourselves.

Consider Tammy and her friend. As a result of open-ing themselves up unprotected, they contacted more than just Tammy's grandfather. They wrestled briefly with a denial spirit. The queer feeling in their stomachs was that spirit's attack on their solar plexus chakra, which is the power center in the human electromagnetic energy field. The spirit was testing to find out whether either of them would yield her physical body to it. The entity came close to success with Tammy. That's why she thought she had fallen asleep. For an instant, that denial spirit had gained a foothold in her physical body, forcing part of her own awareness to vacate.

It is also beyond this book's scope to discuss details of the possession process. It is worth emphasizing, how-ever, that no soul can be displaced from a physical body without that soul's acquiescence. Souls allow denial spirits to take over their physical bodies because they feel helpless and therefore believe that they are power-less to stop it. Tammy and her friend ultimately were able to resist the denial spirit because they had enough sense of their own power not to give in to it.

Many people do not prove so resilient under attack. Geraldo Rivera devoted the May 15, 1990 episode of his show to the topic of possession. A guest described what it was like to live with a son who was possessed. "You have no will. It's just total fear. It controlled me," she said, referring to the being that possessed her child's body and bullied and terrified her.

We believe her when she said she felt she was being controlled by something outside of self. Control over other souls is precisely what a denial spirit wants. It desires control over others because control, not "evil," as traditionally defined, is the true opposite of love. Our Creator loves us without judgments, standards, or expectations—unconditionally, in other words. As souls created out of unconditional love, we possess free will that is truly and totally free, regardless of the conditions imposed by society and its various institutions.

The talk-show guest thus participated in handing over control of her life to that denial entity. So did her son, though to a far greater degree. Similar to girls and women who display the poltergeist effect, neither of them acted consciously in handing over control. They reached the point of allowing a denial spirit into their lives and even their physical being after many, many lifetimes of trying to learn a big lesson about free will and where true responsibility for self begins and ends.

God finally got Moses's attention by enveloping a bush with flames that did not consume it. Many others also require an extreme experience before they will take the hint and wise up.

Chapter 2

Healing, the circle, and the sacred-spiritual have been linked together in societies past and present around the world. One of the few academic studies to examine the circle, focusing on the association between spiritual healing and circles in art, was published as an art history doctoral thesis by Laura Kirkby, PhD. In it, she writes, "The circle is associated with such properties as divinity, strength, protection, benediction, endlessness, power, virtue, the universe, soul, movement, balance, wholeness, sacred space and wisdom, across Tibetan Buddhism, Shamanism, and the visions of Hildegard of Bingen. The circle is associated with spiritual healing because of its singular ability to represent these qualities...."[1]

She outlines how the circle as a spiritual healing archetype is found in the shamanistic cultures of North America's indigenous peoples, such as in the Navajo sand paintings or medicine wheel; in Asia, in the Tibetan Buddhist Kalachakra mandala as the wheel of time; and in Western European Christianity, in the visions of 12th- century German Abbess Hildegard of Bingen, in the labyrinth, and in the rose windows of Gothic cathedrals. According to RestorativeJustice.org, indigenous peoples worldwide have used the circle to address community issues and concerns for millennia. Wood or stone circles can be found all over Europe, with some sites dating back 5,000 years or more.[2]

The most famous of European circles is, of course, Stonehenge, on the plains near Salisbury, England. One of the most intriguing possible uses of this ancient structure is the theory of two archeologists, Timothy Darville and Geoffrey Wainright. They suggest that uses for Stonehenge possibly evolved from a prehistoric observatory or ancient royal burial ground to a healing shrine similar to Lourdes in France, drawing ailing people who wanted to be made whole again: "[A]fter about 2300 BC the emphasis changes and it is a focus for the living, a place where specialist healers and the health-care professionals of their age looked after the bodies and souls of the sick and infirm."[3] They cite the presence of bluestones, excavated and hauled to the site with extraordinary effort throughout many years and regarded by those who mined them as containing sacred healing properties, as a sign of the healing purpose of Stonehenge.

The circular shape of the structure also supports their theory. The bluestones were arranged in a double circle and later surrounded by a circle of larger sarsen stones. Stonehenge and other stone or wood circles are three-dimensional replicas of what Laura Kirkby found in her review of circle art: "The circle as a two-dimensional symbol is the shape that best represents wholeness, and wholeness is what healing is all about," says Kirkby, now a family daycare educator. In her thesis, she also points out that the words *healing* and *sacred* or *holy* have common linguistic roots. "The verb *to heal*, the adjectives *whole* and *holy* all stem from the same Old Saxon root.... Healing can, in the light of this evidence, be *a making whole*, which in itself is an act that is *holy*. Throughout the thesis, *healing* will therefore mean a return towards a state of wholeness or an ideal state of being."[4]

We cannot be certain, but we suspect that an ideal state of being is entirely subjective, and depends on each us of to define it for ourselves. We do know from our work as energy-healers that when any kind of spiritual or emotional healing takes place, then emotional, spiritual, and even physical pain lessen or depart altogether, providing resolution to a greater or lesser extent. This certainly transpired for all of those whose afterlife healing circle stories we discuss in this book.

We have already mentioned that as we practice the afterlife healing circle, we engage the whole self. Our meaning here is neither symbolic nor metaphorical. Many people think of the whole self as body-mind or body-mind-spirit. These ways of defining self, however, omit the emotional part of our being, which is fully one-fourth of the whole self. Our version of the afterlife healing circle won't work unless the physical body, the mental body, the spiritual body, *and* the emotional body are all active. Later we will explain in greater depth how each part of self contributes to the success of the afterlife healing circle. But the very act of bringing the whole self to the circle and using all of it helps make circle participants whole.

We cannot ever hope to be whole if we live out of only part of our being.

European circle traditions may have been lost to mainstream society, but indigenous peoples use the circle to this day for a variety of reasons, and its use has spread beyond these cultures to many corners of society. Initially in Canada and then in the United States and other parts of the world, the "talking circles" of the natives have been adapted to the legal system as justice circles. In these instances, the circle is more than simply a space for victims and perpetrators of crimes to meet and seek some form of restitution/resolution. The wider community also participates, because the crime is regarded as harming not only the victim but also the fabric of the community. Instead of the confrontational approach typical of a trial in a court of law, coming together in a circle enables those involved to "experience each other not as adversaries but as fellow human beings."[5]

Everyone in the circle—the victim and victim's family, the offender and the offender's family, and community representatives, who can be members of the mainstream legal system or others—gets a chance to speak. The process is designed not to exact punishment as revenge, but to bring healing and understanding to both victim and offender, and to empower the community by becoming involved in determining the outcome of a particular case and in addressing underlying problems that may have led to or facilitated commission of the crime.[6]

RestorativeJustice.org has listed these attributes of the circle, which we have also found to be true as we practice our version of the afterlife healing circle:

- Circles draw on our best values.
- Circles help participants respond from one's best self.
- Circles build community.
- Circles create space for deep listening and being heard.
- Circles generate mutual understanding and respect.
- Circles honor all voices equally.
- Circles make decisions by consensus.

⦿ Circles honor the gifts, knowledge, talents, and experiences that each participant brings.[7]

The collaborative rather than confrontational thinking behind these circle principles was also evident in South Africa's Truth and Reconciliation Commission, established in 1995 after the fall of the Apartheid government. During hearings around the country that began the next year, victims and perpetrators of human rights abuses gathered to tell their stories, which were recorded for posterity. A small minority of perpetrators even received amnesty for their crimes instead of punishment, depending on the circumstances. The aim was to avoid an extended cycle of violent retribution on all sides and grant those harmed by human rights violations the dignity of being heard and witnessed by the entire community, including their agressors.[8]

RestorativeJustice.org states, "Participating in circles is inherently transformative, because we experience the world from more perspectives than our own. Drawing on diverse knowledge and experiences, circles generate options and solutions that are often outside the box of conventional thinking and that often go beyond what one person could generate on their own."[9]

⦿ ⦿ ⦿

Something unexpected and remarkable arose out of the healing circles that Meg Jordan, PhD, RN, CWP, began in 1999. Meg is department chair and professor of integrative health studies and somatic psychology at the

California Institute of Integral Studies. She was inspired to set up her healing circles by the justice circles of the First Nations in Canada. Her circles evolved through several format changes, eventually becoming a monthly gathering of a group of Western and alternative healing practitioners. Included are physicians (on rare occasion), psychiatrists, psychologists, chiropractors, naturopaths, Reiki and Ayurveda practitioners, shamans, herbalists, aromatherapists, and others. The focus of their circle is a patient with a chronic condition who has spent a lot of time and money on allopathic and alternative treatments but has not obtained relief. Meg says, "There's no shortage of patients who say to me, 'I've had multiple layers of chronic conditions. If I could really have two hours free with seven practitioners all at one time, I will jump on that.'" As RestorativeJustice.org notes, Meg and the other practitioners in her circle found the experience to be a community-builder. As the practitioners became better acquainted with each other's expertise in the circle and grew to trust each other, they freely deferred to one another when they realized that a particular patient would benefit more from a different approach. They also began referring clients to each other outside of the circle. Meg says that the patients who have been the subjects of these circles have appreciated the members' honesty in assessing whether or not their form of treatment was helpful to them.

Briana, the intuitive counselor and teacher of the circle, points out, "Even though we may not feel it on a practical level, the circle allows us to soften, to become more receptive to seeing things that we might not otherwise see, and hearing things that we might not otherwise hear."

Meg's circles usually address physical issues, but that does not preclude aiding other ailing parts of self. She recalls one circle when a shaman noted the disruption in the patient's auric field and added, "I'm just going to pray to the hole in your heart and see where you have been trying to grieve."

Suddenly the patient began sobbing and said, "No one's ever recognized that within me before."

The psychiatrist in the circle, who had been rolling his eyes minutes earlier, had them opened instead. Previously he had disparaged energy healers, yet he became one of their biggest advocates because of what he witnessed in the healing circle.

"As a medical anthropologist, I've come to respect energy-healing work so much," Meg says.

We're glad to know that more and more members of the allopathic medical and allied professions are open to the benefits of energy-healing. Our version of the afterlife healing circle very much involves energy, which we will redefine in order to explain its connection to the circle, to healing, to spirituality, and to love, which we have already mentioned is present in the afterlife healing circle and is that which opens us to be more receptive when we are in the circle.

The preceding are just a few of the examples of how the circle is being used today as a more community-based and community-directed alternative to traditional ways of doing things, whether it's an alternative to the courts, to time-consuming and costly sequential medical visits, or to redressing the wounds of an entire nation polarized by racial laws. Meg's circles, for example, are considered experimental efficiency models, and she hopes to compile evidence of their efficacy. As such, these circles have not been integrated into the healthcare insurance reimbursement system. "I don't think anyone wants to go that route with it," she adds.

We understand that sentiment entirely. Meg's circles have become a way for adherents and practitioners of many Western and complementary healing disciplines to transcend the isolation they experience in their practices and come together to help a patient and enjoy a community of equals.

According to RestorativeJustic.org, there are at least 20 circumstances in which the use of the circle as an alternative for problem-solving at a personal or community level is appropriate. These include places such as youth centers, businesses and the workplace, prisons, churches, nonprofits, and elder care centers, as well as subjects such as community planning, inmate re-entry into society, veterans' needs, environmental cleanup, recovery from trauma and grief, and support of the dying and their families in hospice.[10] But in all of these examples of how the circle can be a helpful, even trail-blazing alternative, there is no mention of using circles to reach out to the other side—to speak with those not in physical bodies. Our version of the circle is a lot further out of the mainstream than other circles. It all depends on how we define *community*, however. We believe that community is incomplete if it does not include those who are not in physical bodies—the other side. We talk all the time with our spirit guides, who play a key role in the afterlife healing circle, and who most definitely do not have bodies that we perceive as physical. We also work with nonphysical beings during our energy-healing sessions. We consider them our colleagues and beloved friends, and they are no more imaginary than we are.

The other side is a lot closer than many of us realize or perhaps care to acknowledge. Anyone, in fact, can speak to the so-called dead and the not yet born. Later in this book we recount stories of people who did not set out to communicate with the other side, but nonetheless received all manner of communications from souls not in bodies that we consider physical. We will explain how to identify and enhance these intuitive communications, because they happen constantly, even if we do not recognize them as such, and because we need them for the afterlife healing circle to succeed.

🌀 🌀 🌀

According to the well-known Western European myth of Camelot, King Arthur gathered his knights at a circular table. He chose that particular table configuration to foster a sense of equality among his knights by eliminating the head and foot of the more common rectangular table shape. This inevitably produced tension between the ideal of social equality, as embodied in the round table, and the reality of the decidedly non-egalitarian political hierarchy that Arthur led as monarch. Unlike the circle, Camelot did not endure.

Today, we love the circle as a group healing practice for the same reason Arthur did: the shape gives all participants equal standing. As Jean Shinoda Bolen writes in her book *The Millionth Circle*, "...a circle is nonhierarchical—this is what equality is like. This is how a culture behaves when it listens and learns from everyone in it."[11] The circle puts into action our belief in the fundamental spiritual equality of all created souls. "When we circle, the lines of resistance disappear and we are in flow," Meg pointed out. "When we stay in hierarchy, we stay in top-down authoritative lines of inquiry, and deep healing is not facilitated."

We agree. Healing is far more complete and powerful if we play an active role in it. So is our connection to spirit, to God. We do not fare well if we outsource it to others. We have made and are now trying to rectify two huge mistakes: First, we divorced healing from spirituality and tried to leave it solely in the domain of science. It's a classic example of trying to live and function out of only one part of our being—in this case, the mental body. Something huge is missing from the purely scientific model of healing, as many scientists and physicians now acknowledge and are trying to change. Second, and even more insidious and harmful, we outsourced our connection to God and spirituality to top-down hierarchies. Under these systems emerged a class of anointed or appointed priests, pastors, lamas, gurus, masters, and so on, who presumably possessed greater spiritual connections or "pull" than everyone else. Holding themselves out as closer to God, the Divine, or Nirvana (or however each particular religion or faith expresses it), these spiritual overseers then insisted on mediating and dictating to the rest of us the conditions of our relationship with God/Source/Allah/Universal Mind (choose any comfortable label; we prefer the word *God* because it's concise and to the point).

There is an old saying along the lines that if we allow others to do something for us, eventually they will do something *to* us. Never has this proven truer than in spiritual matters. Think back to the recent sexual abuse scandals in the Catholic Church around the globe. Other faiths are by no means immune from such travesties. For example, polygamist Warren Jeffs of the Fundamentalist Church of Latter-Day Saints will spend the rest of his days in prison for raping a 14-year-old child and facilitating more such rapes of underage girls. And in 1993, 80-plus members of the Branch Davidians remained with David Koresh to perish in a fire near Waco, Texas. Similarly, more than 900 members of the People's Temple obeyed the order of their leader, Jim Jones, to kill themselves in Guyana in 1978. Granted, these are extreme examples, but they are the logical outcome of handing over ultimate spiritual authority to anyone or anything other than ourselves, and then hoping to ride to Heaven or Nirvana or wherever on that person's or institution's ostensibly purified coattails. This is dangerous because it strips us of a great deal of our native spiritual power and transfers that power illegitimately outside of ourselves. Loss of personal power and authority is why parents allowed a church leader sexual access to their young daughters. It's why boys and girls remained silent when parish priests sexually abused them. It's why people stayed to die in the flames or drank the Kool-Aid that ended their physical bodies. They gave their spiritual power and authority to someone outside of themselves and thus became vulnerable to abuse and exploitation.

A wise rabbi once told his listeners that the Kingdom of God is within. Jesus was not referring to a physical structure like a church, a mosque, a temple, or an ashram. He was talking about what is within the self, inside the heart and spirit that truly defines who we are as physical, mental, emotional, and spiritual beings. Too many of us, even those who profess to be Christians, act as though we don't believe him. We look everywhere except within for a relationship or connection with the divine. In vesting our trust externally, we give over our power to the rabbi or the priest, the pastor or the imam, the lama or the guru, just as we have handed over healing authority to physicians or political authority to elected politicians.

Tragically, and inevitably, some among them betray us. They cannot help it. They are human, just as we are, and despite all pretensions to the contrary, they don't know anything more about the divine or healing or running a country than the rest of us, and they are no better connected or more insightful than we.

No person and no institution has the right or authority to stand between or define our relationship (or lack thereof) with God/Source/Divine/Universe. No one. Our relationship with God (or whatever you wish to call it) is one of the most critical relationships we will ever have. It is far too central to our wellbeing and wholeness to vest it in someone else's jurisdiction. It is ours alone to nurture and grow, although we are certainly free to seek out help and advice along the way. That's why God didn't stop with Adam in fleshing out creation. We are here to help each other, not step on each other's spiritual toes or order each other's spiritual business. It just so happens that the afterlife healing circle is a moving and beautiful way to help others in need.

We the authors, Jana and Candace, did not start out believing in the fundamental spiritual equality of all created souls. We each came to this place by experiencing our own personal equivalent of that burning yet unconsumed bush. Our life experiences opened us to a greater reality and to reclaiming our personal power so that we could exercise it in a loving, giving manner, such as conducting, participating in, and promoting the afterlife healing circle through this book.

The following chapter relates our stories in brief and how we began to incorporate the healing circle into our practices as energy healers.

Chapter 3

We learned many years ago that community is missing something profound when we do not include our spirit guides as members. By implication, of course, community also includes God, but we'll take this one step at a time.

As it turns out, spirit guides, also known as angels, play a key role in keeping the afterlife healing circle safe and secure. We have come to rely on their love, protection, and practical support not only during the healing circle, but in our daily lives as well. It took a personal crisis, however, for both of us to open up to a larger perspective.

Jana was at her wits' end. The restaurant she owned was failing, she owed the IRS a huge sum of money that she did not have, and her long-term partner had just ended their relationship.

She returned to an empty house at twilight after work one day and hit bottom, in a crisis of despair. She sank to her knees. "There has to be something more," she said out loud, even though no one was in the room with her.

"Are you asking?" a voice said clearly, outside of her head. She was too stunned to respond.

"Are you asking?" the voice repeated in an even more urgent tone.

"I guess I am," she answered finally. *Are you God?* she wondered in silence.

"No," she heard, followed by gentle laughter.

Jana cringed. In her limited understanding, she believed that the only other option was a name she could not bring herself even to think about, much less speak out aloud.

"No, I'm not *him*, either," the voice said. More laughter. It was disconcerting that this invisible stranger could read her mind.

Jana summoned her courage. "Then who are you?"

"I am a friend who has been with you since the beginning of your time," which Jana understood to be the start of her life. "You have many more friends, and when the time is right, I'll be happy to introduce you to the others. My main function is to help you with your spiritual growth."

I'm going crazy, Jana thought.

The room filled with a yellow-white light. Yellow was the color Jana had always associated with unconditional love. Such a love was what she felt now; soft, sweet, warm, gentle, and yet strong. Soon, all that Jana could feel was that love, herself, and that being beside her. She knew that love came as much from God as it did from the voice. Her doubts, fears, and depression melted away.

"What is your name?" she asked.

Dozens and dozens of names flashed before Jana's inner vision.

"I have been all of these names and more over many lives."

"Who were you in your most recent life?"

"I was a member of the Yaqui tribe."

"Then may I call you Yaqui?"

"Yes. I know you have many questions and I will be happy to answer some of them now."

Jana again summoned her courage. "Is God displeased with me?"

"Oh no, my child."

"Then why is *He* doing this to me? Why is my life in such a mess?"

"He is not doing this to you. This was the only way you could bring yourself to ask for help."

That hit home. Jana had never asked anyone for anything. Even as a child, she used baby-sitting money to buy school supplies instead of expecting her parents to pay. Now she was in a position of having to turn to others for assistance. It was humbling.

They talked and talked. Yaqui offered her an entirely new way of thinking and feeling. The only other time she had ever felt this close to the divine was when, as a girl, she had sung hymns in the church choir. She wanted to keep that feeling of connection.

Time passed, but Jana was not aware of her body. Only when Yaqui's love finally faded away did she realize that hours had gone by, and she was still on her knees.

Jana had graduated from high school intending to become a minister of religious education, because traditional religion was the only avenue she knew about at the time. But after her first internship, she realized that was not the route for her. She left college and looked for a job, hoping that work would fill the inner void.

By the time she met Yaqui, Jana had racked up experience in industries that ranged from commercial airlines and hospitals to credit unions and fast food. But the spiritual was never lost, even if Jana did not recognize its presence until Yaqui and her other guides pointed it out to her.

She had always been a counselor, teacher, and healer, even if she did not think of herself that way. Complete strangers were always spilling their hearts and secrets to her and asking her for advice and perspective. She often "career coached" subordinates who were not doing well at or happy with their jobs, with the result that she never had to fire anyone. She was constantly showing her staff how to work better and more efficiently, or being that shoulder to lean on when they had personal problems. All of it was counseling, teaching, and healing, simply without the job titles or traditional degrees.

Jana mentioned her experience with Yaqui to one of her best customers, with whom she often had long talks after the restaurant closed following lunch. The woman told her about a place where she was planning to get some training in developing her intuition and offered to fund Jana's studies. They planned to teach classes together.

Jana went for it. She studied to become an intuitive counselor, a person who uses help from her own and her clients' spirit guides to cut through the confusion and get to the heart of the issue. She learned a healing method that works with the energy of human consciousness and emotions. Next, she trained extensively to teach courses on consciously using the soul or inner senses (also known as psychic abilities), which, like spirit guides, play a key role in the healing circle and any activity that involves spirituality and growth.

Jana has always been eerily good at using her soul senses to tune into what transpires in other people's hearts and minds. In the years ahead, psychologists, licensed professional counselors, business owners, and consultants would come to Jana for advice and perspective whenever they were stumped. When Jana taught a class, did one-to-one counseling, or did therapy with clients individually, her love and the love of Yaqui and her guides would flow through and gob-smack people on the receiving end.

"Who are you?" a soon-to-be client/student asked Jana not long after encountering her at a Seth conference. Jana often heard that question or some variant of it.

"No one special," she always replied. "What I can do, you can do—everyone can do."

During the summer of 1986, Jana still had a day job and was trying to pull together entry-level classes on soul-sense development. In July, one of the students who attended a two-weekend course was coauthor Candace.

🌀 🌀 🌀

Like Jana, Candace had turned to work in an effort to fill that emptiness within. Unlike Jana's variety of jobs in different industries, however, Candace focused on journalism. Putting words on paper was her one marketable skill. For the previous decade, she had been employed full time for daily and weekly newspapers as a copy editor and reporter. At the time of the class, Candace earned a living as a senior editor for an advertising trade publication.

Journalism was even more decidedly male-dominated back in the 1970s through the mid-1980s than it is today. Once Candace specialized in business reporting, almost all of her colleagues and editors were male. Candace had developed a tough professional shell in order to survive and function in the newsroom. Arriving at the *Dallas Times Herald* during the height of its war with its cross-downtown rival, Candace discovered she was good at beating her competitors to stories on her business beats.

Similar to many of her ink-stained colleagues, Candace dreamed of writing and publishing the Great American Novel, or something close to it. A typical introverted wordsmith, she read voraciously in her meager spare time. Although she told herself it was research for that novel she intended to write, it was also her way of exploring what she called the "alternative explanation." Candace never bought into conventional wisdom on anything. In any topic—politics, medicine, history, religion, life in general—Candace didn't take the accepted story at face value. She learned from experience as a reporter that so-called facts are slippery little devils, and that highly prized "objectivity" is more of a myth than unicorns.

Candace was looking for answers—her own answers, ones that resonated with her, not those handed down by some authority. She wasn't looking for a master or a guru or a priest or a pastor to tell her what to believe or how to live. For that reason much of what passed for New Age and New Thought in the mid-1980s didn't interest her, because she regarded it as yet another way to control people. Candace was unabashedly independent.

Her need to do for herself, experience for herself, and find her own answers led her to encounter a program that taught participants about how to recognize and access their psychic abilities for themselves. That suited Candace, because she wasn't looking for a psychic or a medium. Although there were local instructors offering this course, Candace headed more than 50 miles west to the class that Jana was teaching. It was that class that called her name.

When Candace met Jana for the first time and heard her speak, one of the first thoughts that popped into her head was, *She's a lot like Judith*. That was the name of an important character in the novel that Candace intended to write. (Much later Candace discovered that Jana and Judith are indeed one and the same soul.) Candace also saw and felt, vaguely, how easily Jana comprehended her students' real questions, the ones they could not always put into words. Jana chatted breezily about her relationship with her spirit guides, too.

The class accelerated a deep longing within Candace, who, underneath that hard-shell journalist exterior was a gooey mess of unresolved spiritual and emotional pain. She was in a world of hurt and had major emotional problems, although she could not recognize it because her mind and heart were literally disconnected. Candace's guides, however, went straight to Jana and, throughout the course, pleaded with her to do something. Jana also felt the tug of Candace's badly wounded emotional body. Candace's protective cover didn't fool Jana one bit.

After the last class of the first weekend, Jana casually invited Candace down to a floating dock on Eagle Mountain Lake that belonged to the home where the program was being held. What transpired was an impromptu healing session, which moved Candace to agree to the healing method Jana practiced called Sunan therapy. After just six sessions and her first conscious meeting with her own guides, and Candace's emotional and spiritual reality had shifted 180 degrees. Her mental and emotional bodies reconnected, Candace began communicating with her guides daily through automatic writing, which did not (and still doesn't) involve any strange phenomena.

Filled with hope, Candace was determined to help bring Jana's work to a wider audience. The woman Jana originally intended to partner with had become preoccupied with a family crisis. Jana had tried to help her as much as possible, but the woman became more and more wrapped up in a nasty battle and was not in a place to teach. Jana accepted Candace's offer to establish a school where she could devote herself full time to counseling, teaching, and healing. Candace's job provided a base of financial support.

At the outset, Candace was more of an observer and supporter than a participant. She met and liked Jana's students and clients, but was not directly involved in the work, except when Candace undertook more Sunan therapy with Jana as her therapist. That changed, however, when Candace was able to participate in the afterlife healing circle that Jana had scheduled for a Saturday afternoon. Candace was intrigued but had no idea what to expect.

Clara Jones (a pseudonym) was a school teacher who suffered a devastating emotional and spiritual wound that refused to heal for two decades, despite some of the best psychiatric treatment in the world.

Clara was raised in a small Russian Orthodox community in the eastern United States. Her mother and father were first-generation immigrants who, Clara realized later, used their intuitive abilities to survive in a culture they didn't really comprehend. They also kept their Russian background quiet during the days of Joseph McCarthy and Congressional investigations of suspected Communist activities.

"My mother denied her past and lived a facade," Clara said. When her mother died of cancer in 1967, Clara felt she had never had the chance to say goodbye to her real mother.

Five years later, Clara began three years of intensive psychiatric therapy with daily sessions. "I felt like they literally dug me out of a grave," she said of the physicians who attended her. The doctors, however, were unable to help her resolve her feelings about her mother. During therapy, Clara would sense her mother's presence. Feelings that she had lived other lives would also take hold of her. The doctors called it her imagination and dismissed it. They didn't know how to address her spiritual or emotional needs.

Clara tried psychotherapy again in the 1980s and stuck with it for five months. The same thing happened: traditional therapy could help her to a certain point; past that point, it was of no further use to her. "I felt a pressure that no one could help me with," she said. "When your problems touch on the spiritual, traditional doctors can't do much. I had a spiritual injury that I couldn't ignore."

Prodded by her intense and deep-seated need for healing, Clara was open to an alternative approach to grief resolution. Her desire to resolve this issue eventually led her to a counseling session with Jana through Clara's daughter, who was one of Jana's students and had mentioned her mother's problem.

Jana offered to conduct the afterlife healing circle for Clara, who immediately agreed to it even though her daughter had some doubts. "I knew the offer [of the afterlife healing circle] was right. I felt it," Clara explained.

Despite her confidence, Clara was taken aback by the proceedings. "It was shocking when I realized how 'real' it was."

Three years after that afterlife healing circle, Clara told Candace that it enabled her at last to make peace with her mother—two decades after her mother's physical body had died. Clara found that other areas of her life also healed. She felt more at ease with herself and less compelled to be with other people just to avoid being by herself. Equally important to her was that she now had some terms for the intuitive abilities that were always so natural to her and her parents. "It was a tremendous eye-opener to realize the reality of life after death and that other people felt this way," Clara said.

Ironically, it was the healing circle that reconciled Clara to the church of her childhood, which she rejoined not long after her circle. "The church is not open to this subject, but I'm in a whole different space," she said. As a result of the afterlife healing circle, when Clara made the sign of the cross and followed other rituals, she was now aware of a much deeper spiritual dimension. The ceremonies came to hold a rich and very personal meaning for her. She no longer regarded the rites as just motions done by rote and handed down as someone else's truth.

Clara wasn't the only person amazed by her afterlife healing circle. Candace, too, was floored by how much intuitive information she and others received during that circle. Similar to the other participants, Candace was moved to tears of joy and gratitude during the emotional reunion between Clara and her mother. Everyone present experienced and celebrated the reality of life after death.

The effect of this simple proceeding was staggering. Candace had to shake her head and smile, because if anyone had told her just a year earlier that she would be part of something like this, she would have thought this person was crazy and would have said so in no uncertain terms. Not anymore. The afterlife healing circle was precisely the kind of personal spiritual experience Candace so very much wanted and insisted on rather than words handed down from an authority. Indeed, she had never witnessed the presence of God in quite the same gripping and moving manner in which she has experienced it repeatedly during the afterlife healing circle.

Eventually, Jana trained Candace along with other students to be intuitive counselors, using their soul senses and clients' spirit guides to obtain helpful information and to conduct the healing circle when it was appropriate. Jana also trained Candace and others in Sunan therapy, an intuitive approach to resolving deep emotional and spiritual wounds and issues. From time to time, either clients or students of these counselors needed the afterlife healing circle. Candace tried to participate whenever her work schedule allowed, because the afterlife healing circle, for her, was far more moving and powerful than any traditional religious service she had ever attended. It spoke far more eloquently about everlasting life than any sermon ever could, and evoked more joy and faith than any text, however sacred.

When we work as intuitive counselors or energy-healers using the Sunan method, we do not adhere rigidly to any type of system that the left brain might understand or recognize. Members of the Sunan Society explain that the approach they have imparted to us incorporates and blends many ancient and diverse traditions of wisdom and healing that have arisen on earth and elsewhere.

For the purposes of the afterlife healing circle, we can boil the Sunan method down to three simple principles:

1. Love
2. Connection
3. Trust

Love means we know how to send and receive unconditional love. We keep mentioning the presence of love during the afterlife healing circle because it is so critical. We'll explain more about that special kind of love and how it makes the healing circle, as we practice it, both possible and healing.

Connection means simply that we always keep the flow of love open among us, our clients, the invisible healers who are supporting and helping us, and the divine. This definitely applies during the afterlife healing circle.

Trust is really about self-trust. We have enough self-trust that we trust the information about the client that we receive in that flow of love. The information doesn't have to be logical or rational or make sense to us because it's not for us; it's for the client. Trust (in self) is a definite must for the afterlife healing circle, which often reveals to participants information that seems strange because it's not for them; it's for the person they are trying to help.

These principles are tough for many people to apply. They pose a challenge for beginners and even for those who have more experience in our version of the after-life healing circle. But applying these principles is absolutely essential, as Candace was to witness many more times after the amazing circle that Clara found so powerfully healing.

Chapter 4

When we want to contact souls on the other side, most of us usually think about connecting with someone whose physical body has died. Fewer of us realize we may also contact souls who have not yet been born. The same principles of love, connection, and trust apply in both circumstances. And because the soul is a continuum that exists not only in an afterlife, but during a beforelife, too, such communication is possible.

If there is a genuine need to speak with a soul not yet born, we use the afterlife healing circle to make that encounter safe and productive, devoid of drama or phenomena that just get in the way and are not at all helpful.

Debra Wilde (another pseudonym) was trapped in an agony of indecision.

Her eight-year marriage to a man older than she, of another nationality, culture, and religion, had never been easy. Now it was threatening to founder on the shoals of severe financial strain and quarrels over in-laws. At age 29, she already had one child, a daughter nearly 3 years old, and she was pregnant again. This time, Debra couldn't feel the joy so many women experience upon learning this news. She feared the possibility of raising not one but two children by herself. How would she find the courage to give birth again? Should she consider an abortion? The choice was overwhelming. Her husband didn't make things any easier for her. He said the decision was hers and refused to discuss his feelings about the pregnancy, leaving Debra even more isolated and in greater pain.

Then a friend suggested the afterlife healing circle. "I didn't realize you could do one for an unborn child," Debra said. She contacted Jana and discussed the situation, and Jana agreed to conduct a circle for her.

Although her husband didn't believe in "all this metaphysical stuff," as Jana calls it, he accompanied Debra and participated in the session, partly out of curiosity, but mostly out of genuine, although inarticulate, concern for his wife. A couple who were friends of Debra and her husband also took part. Both of them, accomplished professionals, had never done anything like this before. At that time they were just becoming interested in spiritual growth and alternative healing. We always emphasize one point about the afterlife healing circle: We don't have to be professional psychics, or even consider ourselves to have any psychic ability, to take part in and contribute to a healing circle. We need only apply the three principles: love, connection, and trust.

During our afterlife healing circle for Debra, a little soul comes to stand in the middle of our circle, undetectable to the five physical senses but perceptible nonetheless. Tousled dark hair spills out from under a tight-fitting, old-style aviator helmet. He—this soul clearly presents his form as male—is wearing a jumpsuit and a scarf. In the hand that he holds up is a model airplane that dives and loops and curls when he waves his arm. Next to him is what looks like an architect's model of an office building, almost as tall as he.

He is a self-assured soul with a genuine sweetness about him. There is also a hint of mischief and of a very strong will. He knows what he wants for this physical lifetime. He wants to fly airplanes. He tells us he has chosen Debra's husband as a father partly because her husband is a licensed pilot with thousands of hours in the cockpit. He also says he's interested in architecture and designing things.

He has a very full agenda for his next sojourn on earth. He's so cute and bright and cheery that he moves some of us to smiles as we gather this information through our soul senses and pass it on to his would-be mother and father.

Then Debra blurts out a few jumbled phrases. She can barely put her feelings into words to explain to this soul why she is so reluctant just now to continue this pregnancy. Her painful quandary and distress are so palpable, so immediate, that Candace's eyes fill with tears. Others react the same way.

The little aviator quickly understands. "I can wait," he assures Debra several times during the session. "If the time is not right, I'll wait."

Before the afterlife healing circle is over, the little aviator makes sure we all understand one thing: when he finally does arrive, by golly, he wants to be known by his father's middle name.

Candace can't help nodding. The name suits him.

Immediately after her circle, Debra found that the nausea she had been experiencing in the early stages of her pregnancy simply vanished. "My whole attitude changed," she said. "The pregnancy became something I accepted. And it did something else for me; it made me realize that even if my marriage didn't stay together, I still wanted the baby. It gave me more confidence in myself. I'm so glad now I chose to keep the baby. He came to help me with balance."

The afterlife healing circle helped Debra sort through her dilemma. Her marriage ended in divorce, and not long afterward, she sold her business and moved out of state. The little aviator touched down on planet earth the following spring, and is now in his 20s. Debra eventually remarried.

Debra and Clara immensely appreciated and benefitted from the afterlife healing circle, but many others will not. We took some lumps learning this lesson. One of Jana's students introduced an acquaintance who asked for the afterlife healing circle. Jana's intuition waved a big red flag of doubt about this woman's true motives, but she was so insistent and emotionally needy that Jana agreed to do it. That proved to be a big mistake. The woman wanted to communicate with her late husband, not for healing resolution, but to find out where he had stashed a mind-boggling sum of drug money. He was murdered because his drug connections knew he had been holding back on payments. His death was grisly and depressing, as we witnessed it once again during the session.

Even worse, the people who killed him were ruthless and determined to find that money one way or another. Had the woman discovered its whereabouts during the circle, her own physical safety—and possibly the security of all those who participated with her—could have been in jeopardy. Jana called an abrupt halt to the circle before the location of the money could be determined. Even the woman's late husband, once he was in the circle, repeatedly implored her to forget about what he called "blood money" and get on with rebuilding her life. She was less than receptive to that urgent message.

To this date, this has been the only afterlife healing circle involving Candace that evoked complaints afterward from some of the participants. Mostly, they were amazed the woman wanted anything to do with the money. They realized the extreme danger, even if she chose to ignore it. Looking back after many years, Jana suspected the woman took part in her late husband's drug dealings.

Since then we have been even more careful when screening people who ask for the afterlife healing circle. We call such a person the *inquirer*. A request is the first guideline. We make it known that we are capable of conducting the afterlife healing circle and willing to do so, and then we allow an inquirer, such as Clara or Debra, to make a request of us. Next, we establish that the inquirer has some sort of emotional tie to the soul to be contacted *that is reciprocated*. This two-way connection can be through kinship or friendship; it doesn't matter, and we don't need or want to know the precise nature of the relationship. That usually becomes apparent during the circle.

The love connection counts above all else. The emotional bond and recognition are what draw the soul in question to the afterlife healing circle. "When you circle with men and women who are all coming together for a similar purpose, it sends out a beacon...that our ancestors can come and make themselves known," explained Brianna, the intuitive counselor and teacher. "They have a safe space."

Even disembodied souls want and need reassurance about their security. This is obvious, if we think about it. If we were walking down the street and someone in the middle of a group called out our name, would we respond to the summons? We might, if we recognized and cared about the person calling our name. If we didn't know anyone there, most likely we would ignore the call and continue on our way, probably at a little faster clip than before. Unless, of course, we crave attention or, even worse, want to stir up trouble. This is why adoring fans are more likely to contact an impersonator of Michael Jackson, Princess Diana, or Elvis Presley who is no longer in a physical body, not the soul who actually lived as one of these well-known people. The fans hold no emotional draw for any of these three, even if the fans worshipped their idols from afar. Those who might be able to reach the Gloved One, the princess, or the King of Rock 'n' Roll are their family members or close friends. The only way to find out for certain is to conduct the afterlife healing circle with one or more of these people present. The need for a two-way emotional connection between the inquirer and the soul(s) in question helps minimize the inappropriate use of the afterlife healing circle. This simple procedure is most definitely not intended as a means of invading where we have not been invited, even if it is tempting to try to be of service.

Some time ago we discussed more than once the possibility of using the afterlife healing circle for all the souls who remain caught up in a major plane crash near where we live, but we don't stand much of a chance of being successful without involving at least one person with a very close emotional tie to someone whose physical body perished in the accident. We are not acquainted with anyone in that situation, and no such person has come forward to ask us for help. If such a person were to agree to act as the inquirer, then that person might be able, with the help of a group, to attract the attention of at least one soul. Then we could all help that soul realize that the pain is over and that it is free to move on. That soul, in turn, might be able to get other souls still lingering at the crash site to come to the group to hear the same message. The group would also help set them free and show them the way to the light of God's unconditional love.

That is what is known as a *soul rescue*. It is one of the most loving and generous acts any of us can do for someone else. Even so, we need the permission and participation of someone affected by the situation.

@ @ @

At first, Jana thought her client was exaggerating in her description of the circumstances that bothered her. The woman was worried about the physical safety of her house and her neighbors' dwellings, too. The more the client talked about her unsettling visions, and once Jana tuned in to the situation using her intuition, she realized that there were souls around her client with issues that the afterlife healing circle could help resolve. A soul rescue could be done. Candace made phone calls and arranged for a group of clients and students to meet at the woman's house one fall evening.

Many years after the circle we're about to describe, Yaqui explained to us that these souls were a breakaway group of cliff-dwelling Native Americans from the desert southwest. Men, women, and children, walked east many hundreds of miles looking for a place where they could rebuild their lives and live in peace. Eventually they arrived at a low-lying locale near a source of water and set up a temporary camp. They intended to move on because they knew they were crossing disputed territory claimed by several tribes, and it was not safe to linger, but seemed a good spot to stop and take an extended rest, hidden from prying eyes.

They were not concealed well enough. Attackers caught them by surprise and slaughtered every one of them, leaving their bodies where they fell to rot under the sun, untended and unburied. The land, soaked with their blood, eventually claimed their bones. Later their remains were covered over by the houses of what grew into one of the affluent cities next to Dallas, Texas. It was as though these people had been washed away and never even existed on this earth.

Lost and seemingly forgotten, they remembered and waited, unwilling to depart despite the entreaties of their ancestors urging these souls in limbo to move into the light.

Leading the afterlife healing circle, Jana is astonished by how many souls gather on the outside of the circle formed by the volunteers and the client. She feels their presence as a tremendous pressure. She says, "All the souls who lived in this area and are upset and not free, please come into the circle." Only one of them enters, and her impression of him is of an older Native American man chosen to be the spokesman for the hundreds and hundreds who are present.

She feels the man vacillate between rage and deep sadness. His rage is from the disrespect shown to his body and the bodies of his family and his tribe. *What soulless thing could have done this?* Jana feels him ask repeatedly. He has been trying to understand for what those in physical bodies would consider many, many lifetimes.

What has infuriated the elderly man and his tribe is not the killing of their physical bodies, Jana realizes. They knew they were trespassing and accepted both the risk and the consequences. They would have done the same to those who encroached on their hunting grounds, because such actions took food out of their mouths and the mouths of their families and tribe. What keeps them livid, unable to move on, is the disrespect shown to their bodies, which were not given the proper rites. The ultimate insult is all of the construction on top of what these souls consider sacred ground where the dead lie, unacknowledged. They find the situation intolerable, soulless, and cannot let it go and depart.

Then one member of the circle sends the old man a huge shot of love, telling him, "You're right. They were soulless. But I don't think they knew you had ever been here. We certainly didn't."

"We acknowledge your presence now and honor you with our love and respect," Jana adds quickly. Beyond the circle she perceives the loving light and the voices of their ancestors, still calling out to them, still urging those who linger to join them. They have been waiting a long time for their loved ones.

Jana asks the group to help her encourage these trapped souls to move through the circle to the light. At long last, it is enough. Their anger subsides enough for them to perceive the light and their ancestors, ready to welcome them home. As they move through the circle, their energy feels like a hurricane to Jana.

"Go in peace," Jana and the other members of the circle tell him and all of the other souls who finally can leave this place to move into the light and into a new life. The old man, the last to depart, looks every member of the circle in the eye and nods his thanks to each one.

In the case of this healing circle, although the client did not personally know the souls in question, she had an intimate connection to them, thanks to the location of her home on the ground where their bodies had fallen and decayed. Without such a legitimate tie, we have no right to butt in, however well-meaning our intentions. The road to we-know-where is paved with good intentions, and we have had no intention of heading in that direction.

Chapter 5

We truly have no desire to encounter the scary or the bizarre during the afterlife healing circle. To keep the experience positive, uplifting, and safe, we are as careful about our motives for conducting one in the first place as we are about the motives of those asking for the circle.

The safest motive for offering the afterlife healing circle is to be of service to others—nothing more and nothing less. More dicey motives might be to entertain, to defraud, or to demonstrate how truly spiritual we are. We most likely would experience negative consequences if we offered the circle with any variation of the latter three as our primary intent.

As mentioned in Chapter 4, the motives of those who ask for the afterlife healing circle are equally important to its safety and success. We conduct the afterlife healing circle only when there is a genuine need for healing resolution between a soul in a physical body and a soul who is not.

The situation of Clara and the client who needed a soul rescue are typical. People usually want to reach someone who has left the physical world, someone we think of as dead. Yet what works for the so-called deceased also applies to those not yet born into the physical, as Debra and other soon-to-be parents have discovered.

Rondi was 40 years old and had suffered multiple miscarriages. Around January of 1993, she went through yet another such experience and believed she no longer was pregnant. Yet her body never really got back to normal; her uterus seemed to keep expanding. Finally, about April, Rondi went to the doctor and had a sonogram to reveal what was transpiring inside of her.

She was still pregnant—with twins!

Rondi was happy, but her husband, Marc, was in a state of anxious shock. He already had two teen boys by his first marriage and wasn't certain he was ready to go through caring for infants again. Mostly he was scared. He lost his first wife to complications from childbirth and could not help fearing the worst this time, given Rondi's age for a first birth. She also had concerns about her physical condition and how the pregnancy was going to work out. They asked for the afterlife healing circle and Jana agreed. On the appointed day Candace participated, too.

It takes a bit of coaxing to bring the first twin into the circle. "She feels very large," Marc says.

This soul presents herself as a fully grown, very determined young woman. "She wants you to know she's as old as you are," Jana tells her parents. We all laugh.

Candace understands intuitively that her name is very important to her, so we ask her what she wants to be called and she guides us to a choice she finds acceptable.

"What is it you wish your mother and father to know?" Jana prompts her.

This soul loves her mother's heart, and tells Rondi that she is far more loving than she has given herself credit for being.

"Quit worrying," the soul adds through Jana. "You can't screw up. It takes two to learn and two to share."

The soul's deep emotions touch all of our hearts. She turns to Marc, who, she says, was her father in a previous life. "You weren't as open to your heart then as you are now," she explains through Jana, "and she always desperately wanted to have your love and could never feel it. She can now."

Everyone's eyes fill with tears.

This soul's purpose for this physical life? To love with hope, not attachment, and to help others learn to do the same.

"In what way would you express that?" Jana asks.

In every way, she replies, showing Candace an image of a young woman spreading seeds of joy and nurturing them with her watering can.

Her life's lesson is learning patience and sharing with joy, love, and compassion. That is one of the reasons she is coming into the world with a twin.

"Intense," her father says about her.

"No, powerful," Jana suggests. "She has a sense of humor that intense people tend not to have."

The soul also explains she needs to learn more about self-love and how to balance being a spiritual being with a physical being. She asks both of her parents for help with this lesson.

"She again says she is grateful for your acceptance," Jana tells Marc and Rondi. "You could have chosen otherwise."

"Is there anything I can do to make you feel more welcome or healthier?" Rondi asks.

Her parents' warm welcome is enough for her. She tells them not to worry about her health, because she is strong, but she does have concerns about her brother, whose physical body does not have the same stamina as hers.

"Take care of yourself," she urges Rondi. "I want a healthy mother."

"So do I," Marc chimes in quickly.

Jana asks her to step outside the circle so that her brother may enter and speak to their parents. Instead, she brings him inside and hovers close by, protecting him. Unlike his out-front sister, this soul radiates a gentle, soft energy, similar to a summer breeze. He offers two strong names, and his parents suggest an adaptation of one of them, to which he agrees.

"Such a sweet energy," Jana whispers. "Go ahead and embrace your mother and father."

Rondi sobs and Marc clears his throat.

"He says, 'I love you.' He's been with you before, a little role reversal here. He's been your father."

"Why did you choose us this time?" Rondi manages to inquire.

"Because you needed me and she [his sister] needs you," he explains through Jana. This soul already understands unconditional love and will help his parents with self-love. The boy asks his parents to treat him and his sister as individuals, not as twins. He specifically requests that his mother, a vegetarian, consume more protein during her pregnancy. "Just talk to me," he also tells her. "You're always talking to her [his sister]. She's just louder. Ask me directly—you'll be able to hear me."

His purpose for a physical life is to be a pathfinder for others as a means of finding his own way. "He has a natural bent for fixing things, for taking them apart and putting them back together," Candace intuits. "Watch your car."

"He's a tinkerer of things—and a tinkerer of philosophy," Jana adds.

This soul will need his parents' help in learning to verbalize his emotions. His twin will want to speak for him but she needs to step back and let him find his way. "He wants you to take the time to draw him out," Candace tells his father.

The parents are concerned about the birth, and he reassures them that he and his sister will make it as easy as possible for their mother during labor and delivery, and will probably arrive two to three weeks early. He also reassures them that he will reach out to their older brothers and help them understand their sister better. They wonder about Rondi's miscarriage early that year. He explains that there was a third soul that opted not to continue with the pregnancy. They could have chosen younger parents, Jana points out, but wanted maturity—parents who have already met some of the same desires they have set for themselves.

She asks each soul to enter its fetus to give their mother a boost of energy, which Rondi feels and reports.

"I just want to tell them both how much we love them," she adds through more tears. "It's going to be an incredible experience for all of us."

The rewards of the afterlife healing circle for Rondi and Marc went far beyond some much-needed reassurance that Rondi's pregnancy and birth would be safe. (The twins are now in their 20s.) Getting to know the two even before they came out of the womb helped their parents be more relaxed and confident about bringing up their children. "To know some of their quirks and their energy before they were born was very freeing," Marc said. "It was now not a process of trying to discover who your kid is. We already knew them."

"It was an allowing," Rondi elaborated. "It gave us permission to just allow them to be who they are without trying to mold them into something."

The afterlife healing circle also aided Rondi in another profound way. She tended to be quiet and not express herself, but after the circle, she became even more open to her own heart and to demonstrating her feelings more freely. "It definitely had the effect for me of being a more emotional person," she explained. "Feeling that love connection was so incredibly strong. That's something I'll never forget."

In the years following their circle, Rondi and Marc have described the experience of the afterlife healing circle to friends who are open to the concept of soul communication, and urge other expectant parents to hold the afterlife healing circle to meet their offspring before birth.

"This is something you need to do for your kids," Marc emphasized, pointing out that it can help parents-to-be prepare for challenges such as a child with a physical or mental handicap, instead of being surprised and assigning blame.

"I don't see how there could be abuse or anything negative because you have such a different perspective going through the experience [of the afterlife healing circle]," Rondi agreed.

We heartily endorse their viewpoint about the extraordinary value of the circle for expecting parents. It's one of the reasons we wrote this book.

In addition to resolving grief and helping parents-to-be, the afterlife healing circle can be helpful in other difficult circumstances such as miscarriage, abortion, or suicide. Many of us regard such events as the end of a budding life, and even murder. What miscarriage and abortion really mean is delay. In both situations, the soul will opt not to return to a physical body, find another mother and father, or wait until the time is better for the woman who was pregnant.

The third option is what happened for a woman we will call Lori Dell. At age 19, Lori, an Oregon resident, became pregnant after her birth control failed. With sexual and other abuse in her past, and needing to do much more work on her own healing, Lori was not emotionally equipped at that point to be a parent, and neither was her boyfriend. She did not want to give birth and put the child up for adoption, either. It was simply too much for her, too overwhelming.

Two months after she chose an abortion, Lori was at her boyfriend's house for a weekend away from college. Asleep that Saturday night, she had a vivid dream. "I hesitate to even call it a dream, because there was something far more real about it," she said.

In that dream, she gave birth to the child, who was a girl. "It's like the air spoke, and told me her name was Ashley." A nurse tried to hand her the newborn, but she refused. "I wouldn't touch her. I couldn't take her. I could not find it in myself to accept her," Lori recalled. So the nurse gave the infant to her boyfriend, who sat down to hold the child. "He was in love with her instantly."

The dream skipped forward and the little girl was about 3 years old, a beautiful child with long blond curls. She and Lori were walking together down a street lined with little shops. They stopped to enter one of them. "Something in me just wanted to tell her how much I loved her and how sorry I was," Lori said. "But I couldn't speak. It wouldn't come out.

"She turned toward me and looked me right in the eye and said, 'It's okay, Mommy. I understand.' She went on into the shop, and I woke up. I remember the incredible sense of joy and peace. I really wanted to hang onto that."

Later that day, Lori learned that her boyfriend had experienced the first part of the dream the prior night, too, after he supplied her with exact details she had left out of her description of her dream to him.

After her abortion, Lori struggled with confusion and mixed feelings. The dream message from the soul that wanted to be her daughter provided some help, but when Lori later became pregnant with the daughter she gave birth to, those painful feelings resurfaced, much to her surprise. When this daughter arrived in the physical world, Lori's mother-in-law kept calling the newborn Grace, which was not the name she was given ultimately. But the word rang a bell for Lori, who regarded the child as a second chance to have a daughter, her "saving grace."

In the shower one morning, it occurred to Lori that her daughter was the same soul as Ashley, whom she thought of at the time as her saving grace because even though it was unwanted, the pregnancy moved Lori to take stock of her life and do some work on herself. Once Lori made the connection between the two daughters, her mother-in-law never again referred to the child as Grace. That seemingly strange incident of a short-term name was this soul's way of helping her mother to realize that she had come back to her and was now growing up.

Not all who suffer through a miscarriage or choose to end a pregnancy have help from a loving soul who knows how to communicate in order to ease her parents' hearts and spirits. In such cases, the afterlife healing circle can be enormously beneficial. It enables both sides to sort out their feelings and say what they want to say but previously believed they would not ever have a chance to.

Sudden infant death syndrome (SIDS, or crib death) is an excruciating event often caused by a soul having a change of heart about the physical life it chose. The soul removes its energy from the infant's physical body, which then dies from causes that medical science still cannot pinpoint with certainty, although there are a number of theories. The anguish that ensues after crib death can be alleviated through the afterlife healing circle. It allows the parents to obtain answers for the seemingly unanswerable question of "Why?" and arrive at a deeper understanding that they are not to blame.

The same applies in cases of suicide. In the circle, the soul(s) in body and those on the other side have the chance to arrive at answers they find healing. We hope that, if nothing else, this book makes clear that suicide does not stop the pain, because the pain is emotional and spiritual, not just physical. We can kill an ailing physical body, but the wounds in the heart and spirit remain unresolved by the physical body's demise.

Please note also that we talk about answers, not *the* answer. There is no one answer that fits all when it comes tothe profound issues of life and death, being and love. As we have explained, the afterlife healing circle provides subjective answers to help people obtain resolution for their unique circumstances and relief for their singular emotional and spiritual pain. That's all it can ever be, but that's more than enough, in our opinion.

So far we have mostly discussed the efforts of those in physical bodies to contact souls who are not embodied, but very often the opposite is what occurs. Those who are not in a physical body, like Lori's once and future daughter, can take the initiative because they also have a need to connect and explain.

The next chapter shows that although such attempts can be successful, they are often haphazard and harder than they have to be because both sides do not quite know how to establish a good connection or how to make the most of it once they do. The afterlife healing circle as we practice it is ideal to solve these kinds of problems.

Chapter 6

Unlike the shy twin from Chapter 5, not all souls who lack a physical body are reticent about making their presence known to those who do have one. Indeed, the so-called dead often take the initiative and reach out to the so-called living first, as do the not-yet born.

We put that modifier in front of the words *dead* and *living* because they start to have very different meanings once we experience the afterlife healing circle. It dawns on us that what seems like a stark divide between physical life and a vast unknown—the other side—may not be such an unbridgeable, unfathomable chasm after all.

As Briana pointed out in Chapter 2, people from pre-industrial societies were much more aware on this subject than we moderns, with all of our emphasis on logic, reason, and technology. They knew their ancestors were still with them in a very real sense because, unlike us, they did not cut themselves off from that wider awareness and community that the afterlife healing circle is designed to recapture and put to good use. Even today, indigenous peoples tend to be closer to the other side and more open about it than people in industrialized nations.

One truth that astonishes those who are separated from spirit is that the "dead" and the not yet born have things they want to tell us, and they do not always wait for us to wise up and notice them. They find what seem like strange ways to get their messages across precisely because we are not paying attention and because we inaccurately think we lack the ability to communicate with the other side.

One day a woman we'll call Barbara Strong answered the telephone. Her friend, John, was on the other end with something to tell her. It seemed fairly mundane except for one slight wrinkle: John had been dead for eight years! Leukemia claimed his life back in 1967, just two days after Barbara's second child was born.

"I was shocked," the Texas resident and retired technical documentation writer said. "He told me something important. Naturally, I thought I would remember that to my grave. I don't."

One day when the phone rang for Barbara's sister, Kate Strong (also a pseudonym), the machine showed that the call was from the assisted living facility where their mother lived. It happened not long after Barbara's and Kate's father had passed on. Kate answered, but no one was on the other end of the line. She tried phoning her mother and got no response. Next she dialed the number displayed by caller ID and was told that no one from the residence had tried to phone her. The staff offered to check up on her mother, but Kate decided to do so herself. She found her mother in her bedroom with an arm wedged between the bed and the wall so tightly it was bleeding from her efforts to free herself.

"In my mind, it was definitely Daddy calling to let me know Mother needed help," Kate said.

Kate's deceased father has reached out to her in other ways, too. Right after his funeral in Austin, Kate and her husband, Jack, were driving home. Looking at the clouds out of the car window, Kate asked silently, *Daddy, if you're okay, send me a sign in the clouds.* Instantly realizing she wouldn't be able to make out anything she wanted to see, she altered her request: *Daddy, send a sign to Jack instead.*

She casually suggested that her husband scan the sky at the next red light. "See what you can make out."

At the next signal, Jack did as she asked. "Wow!" he exclaimed. "I see a great big boat."

"That was Daddy's thing," Kate said of the cloud's shape. "I knew he was all right and didn't have to worry anymore."

The dead calling? This experience is by no means unique to Kate and Barbara. One Friday, the daughter of California resident Marie Rhodes relayed a phone message. It concerned a dear friend who was suffering from a lengthy terminal illness. "Marshal is going to die on Saturday," the communication stated. "He wants you to go with his wife to his daughter's college graduation ceremony."

The next day, Saturday, the phone rang twice. The first two times there was silence on the other end. "The third time I was called," Marie said, "it was to tell me that he had died and I would need to tell his wife. He did not want us to return but to continue on to the graduation."

Marie, many of whose family and friends have died, finds that the so-called dead are just as unpredictable as the living. "Those I do think I will hear from I do not," she said. "I am often surprised by those I do hear from."

No one was more surprised by a visit from the departed than Richard Smith, a pseudonym for a Florida-based counselor. Around 1980, he was sitting in his living room a few days after the death of a man who had come to him for several counseling sessions, at the request of the man's daughter, who was Richard's friend. It was the day of the man's funeral. Suddenly Richard noticed the odor of freshly dug earth. Then he perceived the dead man's presence in his home. The man was distressed because he had not been able to tell his daughter something before he passed on. He wanted Richard to transmit his words to her. Although reluctant and feeling awkward, Richard agreed to the request. The presence and the smell instantly vanished. A few days later Richard relayed to the daughter what her father had asked of him. She started to cry. Richard learned that she had not been able to reach her father's bedside in time. What Richard just told her now was the very same message that her family said the man had given them before he died. "I don't remember the exact message anymore, but I'll always remember the experience," Richard added.

The first communication Astrid, the inspirational speaker we met in Chapter 1, received from her dead father occured when she was in the shower. This is where she prays and talks to God every morning. "I heard someone tell a joke," she said. "It was so sudden, so out of the blue, and so unrelated to what I was thinking, it took me a moment to acknowledge the probability that it could be my dad."

Another memorable message from the departed happened periodically over a number of years to one of Jana's counseling clients we'll call Rebecca Winston. Living alone, Rebecca kept finding blood on the bed sheets. At first she naturally thought it was her own. Yet when these stains appeared, she would examine herself and find nothing that could account for the blood. Finally, she had a sample tested at a laboratory. It proved to be one of the rarest of blood groups. Even more baffling and unnerving, *it was not Rebecca's blood type.* (We'll talk more about Rebecca's story later.)

The not-yet-born also resort to dramatic ways to reach out to their would-be parents. Connecticut resident Marianne O'Hare happily hit the sack one night at 8:01 p.m. Her job at the time as an early morning radio show host meant she had to rise at 3 a.m. on work days. Tonight she was looking forward to getting more sleep than usual.

Suddenly, a shimmering beam of light appeared before the foot of the bed. "It was like nothing I ever encountered before," she said. "I panicked but was unable to move any part of my body." The light filled the room, and out of that light appeared a girl about 8 years old, a glowing light-being fully formed.

"Her arms were outstretched toward me in a kind of appeal," Marianne continued. "Telepathically she asked me if I would 'accept her.' I was terrified at what was happening and still couldn't move my body. I was able to telepathically communicate back to her, 'I don't know who you are. You could be the Devil disguising yourself as a beautiful child.'"

"Look at me," she replied. "Look at my face."

Marianne believed she had no choice except to do as asked. "In that moment, I felt the weight of such a love as I have never known. It was unbelievably beautiful and ethereal and the kind of love folks report in near-death experiences."

"Now will you accept me?"

"I will accept you."

The shimmering figure floated toward Marianne, through her, merging into her being through the left arm. The room went dark and Marianne gasped, finally able to move again.

Trembling, she looked at the clock. The time read 8:01. "The laws of physics, time, and space had just been shaken to their core in my world."

Marianne phoned a sympathetic friend and recounted what had just transpired. "That was your daughter asking permission to be born," the friend replied instantly.

Marianne was not so certain. She did not believe she would be able to become pregnant. The days and weeks passed and the encounter receded into her memory. The next spring, several months later, Marianne noticed her periods were irregular and went to the doctor. She was pregnant, and there was a heartbeat to prove it!

Right up until giving birth on Halloween 1989, Marianne kept thinking she would have a boy. "I remember being surprised to hear, 'It's a girl!' The next instant I remembered the girl child emanating from a beam of light right in front of me. When she opened her eyes and looked at me for the first time, I realized this baby was that child."

The ethereal child is now a young woman who looks very much like the little girl who came to her mother asking to be born.

Not all pre-birth bulletins are so intense or so brief, according to our earthly time reference. Some take longer before coming to fruition.

Rayni Joan was 39 and had two children. She and her husband had decided their family was complete. One summer, the family was on vacation at the beach in the Hamptons. Rayni's husband was wind surfing, and her two boys were playing in the sand. Rayni was sitting under a clear blue sky with one puffy cloud overhead. She looked up at it and heard a voice. "I want to be born to you, Mommy," the voice said.

Her husband did not believe her, but for two years, the author kept hearing the voice, which she knew belonged to a little boy. Throughout those two years she pleaded with her husband for a third child. Finally, in exasperation, Rayni silently told the voice, *Go tell your Dad!* Although her husband did not hear a voice, he suddenly agreed to have another child. Less than a year later, Rayni, at 43, gave birth to her youngest child, a son now in his 20s.

Deborah Frueh, an Illinois-based intuitive coach, told us a similar story. Many months before her fourth and last child was born, she remembers, "I was well aware that he was sitting on my shoulder very insistently." Trying to start a catering company that offered healthy menus, Deborah had mixed feelings about this signal that another child was on the way. "I didn't really think the timing was good for a new baby on top of a new business that I hoped would be all-consuming." Deborah went on, "I kept telling myself it was a manifestation of the new business I was 'giving birth to,' but deep down I knew it was another child, and he was born about a year later."

Deborah believes her son signaled his impending birth to try to spare her the effort of launching a new business that ultimately went nowhere. "For about a year or so, when people saw my newborn child, they would reflexively call him 'Little Buddha,'" she said. "To this day he is my 'seeker' child, always calling me to discuss philosophy and new thought."

In addition to alerting parents to their pending arrivals, children often want their parents to know what to name them. To the son of Sharón Wyeth, a community college math professor in Texas and the author of a book about names, his name was really important. Unaware she was carrying a child, one night years ago Sharón dreamed that her first child came to her and told her his name, which she understood to be Joshua Jedediah. When she woke up the next morning, Sharón found out that her husband had had the same dream; he got a different name, but deferred to her interpretation. A few weeks later, they learned she was pregnant and began referring to the child, whom they knew would be a boy even before the sonogram, as Joshua Jedediah.

Two weeks before the birth, her husband had another dream in which the soon-to-arrive boy admonished him, "Why are you listening to her? She didn't get it right. I don't want my middle name to Jedediah. I want it to be Jeremiah." After her husband reported his second dream, Sharón agreed to call the boy Joshua Jeremiah.

A couple of years later, it was late at night and her husband was away. Sharón was working on an art project when her toddler son, waking from sleep, walked in quietly and startled her. Out of the blue he said, "I came to you and gave you my name, but you didn't get my name right so I had to go to Dad and give him my name. And then I had to go to Dad again because he thought you had gotten it right and he had not."

Sharón's eyes grew wide. Neither parent had ever mentioned their pre-birth dreams to their little boy, thinking he was too young to understand. "Well, you ended up with your right name, so we're good," she managed to reply. Joshua Jeremiah was not finished with his grilling, however. "When are you going to let the other two come through?" he asked.

"What are you talking about?"

"You let me come through and you let my sister come through. When are you going to let the other two come through?"

"I looked at him and said, 'Honey, I'm choosing not to have more children. I'm a school teacher. I deal with kids all day long. When I come home, I have just enough time and energy for you and your sister. I don't think I could do as good a job with four. I think I'm done.'"

"Oh," he replied, and walked away.

Joshua Jeremiah had no way to know that years before, his mother, very much wanting four children, had carefully crafted four Christmas stockings for her offspring and put them away for the future.

Pre-birth name instructions can come even from adopted children. Roughly a month after Austin, Texas residents John and Kathy Wilczek turned in their final adoption paperwork, Kathy had a vivid dream in which she heard, loud and clear, "Olivia is coming!"

The next morning Kathy sat outside as poetry poured out of her mind and heart and onto many pages. She was not a poet. Eight months later, Kathy's narrative book was presented to a young woman and her boyfriend, who chose them to be the parents of a little girl born a bit sooner than expected. When the adoption counselor called and asked what John and Kathy wanted to name their new daughter, they replied in unison, "Olivia!" During the infant's christening, the minister read Kathy's poetry. "The children that are meant to come to us find a way," Kathy told us.

We have been talking a lot so far about communicating with discarnate beings and about perception that clearly does not involve only our five physical senses. Shortly we will review how it is all possible, and how and why the soul is an eternal continuum that we may contact after physical death or before physical birth.

Chapter 7

Haphazard, random, confusing messages from those not in physical bodies raise more questions than they answer. Remember some of the examples we've shared: If it wasn't Rebecca's blood on the sheets, then whose was it? Who or what did Marianne see all those years ago at the foot of her bed? Who or what phoned Barbara, Kate, and Marie? Who or what visited Richard? Who or what managed to provide all those special effects and answers, even though the second stager was locked out of the house during the Grosse Pointe séance? Who or what announced her name to Kathy and her husband, John?

The answer is so simple that most of us find it hard to believe. The *only* thing we leave behind at death is the physical body. That's all. That's it. The rest of self—our mental, emotional, and spiritual self-awareness (our consciousness, in other words)—remains intact. Ghosts, spirits, and apparitions are nothing more, or less, than souls that lack physical bodies to anchor them into what we perceive as the only reality, the physical world. The same applies to all of us before we are born into physical bodies.

The soul, in essence, consists of energy. That is why the soul precedes the appearance of a physical body, which itself is energy in material form, and survives its death. There just so happen to be two mathematical equations to express both death and birth (creation). The first of these is $E = MC^2$. Most of us know this as Albert Einstein's famous equation, published in 1905, stating the fundamental equivalence between matter and energy. It can also describe the process we refer to as death if we alter the equation's variables slightly.

E still stands for energy, although we will refine the meaning of "energy" shortly. M still stands for matter. But instead of the speed of light multiplied by the speed of light (the speed of light squared), C^2 now stands for the duality of consciousness. And the speed of consciousness is instantaneous, as multiple experiments with the tiniest known particles, called *quanta*, have demonstrated. It is way beyond the scope of this book to explore all of the very exciting developments in the fields of quantum mechanics and consciousness research; suffice it to note that the scientific community is moving toward a distinctly metaphysical understanding of the survival of consciousness after death as strings of quanta. One key characteristic of quanta is that they vibrate. Everything that exists—the material, such as the physical body, and the nonmaterial, such as consciousness—vibrates. Every known or theoretical universe vibrates, or else it does not exist. Vibration is the foundation of creation.[1]

For the purposes of the afterlife healing circle, we also need to recognize that whereas the soul is energy, this energy is not the type that science refers to as "the ability to do work." Such a definition applies to *material* energy in this physical world. Examples of this include steam expanding to drive a piston that turns the wheels of a train engine, or the heat unlocked by burning coal or natural gas that raises the temperature of water until it becomes steam. That is "doing work" in the scientific sense.

The soul is not about *doing* work or anything else. The soul is about *being*. It is about existing instead of not existing. The kind of energy that forms the soul is most accurately defined as *the ability to love*.[2] Being and self-awareness, or consciousness, originate in love, the ultimate source, also known as God or the divine in most of the world's religions.

Divine love is unconditional, meaning it is not limited or hampered by expectations or demands. Thus, it vibrates at the fastest frequency possible at any given instant. It also has many names on earth: Hindus call it *prana*, the life-force; the Chinese long ago named it *chi* or *qi*; and Christian Westerners refer to it as *agape*, or divine grace. When we are conducting the afterlife healing circle properly, we are experiencing a magnified, enhanced flow of that unconditional love-energy. As we have said already, the feeling is glorious.

Now we may reinterpret Einstein's equivalence equation. With our redefined variables, we can see that consciousness accelerates in frequency until it breaks away from matter (the physical body). The physical body dies as a result, and consciousness remains in a state that cannot be detected with our physical senses, much like infrared light, which human eyes cannot see, or infrasound, which human ears cannot hear.

If we rearrange these same redefined variables, we can develop an equation to show the process we know as birth, or creation:

$$E = \frac{M}{C^2}$$

Matter (such as a physical body) appears when consciousness acts to slow the vibrational frequency of soul energy. The answer to the question "Which comes first, the chicken or the egg?" is *neither*. Energy comes first, and provides the blueprint for everything that exists in material form. The full equivalence in Einstein's equation, however, comprises far more than matter and energy alone. It also extends to consciousness and *love*. These four—matter, energy, consciousness, and love—are equivalents, and all four vibrate or they would not exist.

Expanding the reinterpreted equivalence equation explains why the presence of love is the key to the success of the afterlife healing circle. Love is both electric and magnetic, giving and receiving, push and pull (attracting). Love, especially love from a person in a physical body with whom the soul is familiar, helps draw the right soul to the circle. Love offers the reassurance that encourages the soul to remain for resolution that usually is much needed on both sides.

🌀 🌀 🌀

After death and before birth, consciousness (or soul-energy, if you prefer) is so intact that even when the physical body is abruptly destroyed, through accident or murder, for example, the remaining self-awareness often doesn't realize what has happened. One example of this is the souls of those killed in the airplane crash for which Jana and Candace considered attempting a soul rescue. An undetected wind shear slammed a jumbo jet violently to the ground just north of the airport runway it was approaching to land. While the physical bodies were removed from the crash site, many of the souls remained for a long time, caught up in that trauma.

Consciousness can indeed be oblivious to the destruction of the physical body. This leads to a lot of seemingly strange events that we usually misinterpret and then label as "paranormal activity." Hauntings are one example. A soul or group of souls may wander around in a state of confusion, unaware of their physical demise. No longer focused in physical reality, such souls don't have the same sense of the passage of time as do those still dwelling in physical bodies. That's why these souls linger in one location (a house or near a runway) for years or even centuries.

Already disoriented or traumatized, these souls become even more bewildered when they realize their families and friends no longer seem to notice them or pay attention when they try to communicate. They may be feeling the extremes of very strong emotions, such as terror or anger. Remember, nothing dies except the physical body. Disembodied souls are as capable of emotions and feelings as anyone reading this page. And it is the energy of very intense emotions that interacts with physical objects, sometimes unwittingly, and at other instances intentionally. Such interactions are known as *psychokinesis*, which produces phenomena such as phone calls from the dead, apparitions, boat-shaped clouds, or the smell of dirt inside a room where none is evident. These events are often prompted by a soul who very much desires to communicate with someone still in a physical body but who cannot get that person's attention in a less disruptive manner.

Often, after someone has passed on to the nonphysical, we have thoughts about that person that seem to pop into our heads from nowhere. Or that individual just seems to be on our mind a lot, even though it may have been years since that person died. If more of us realized what was really going on, we would recognize that this supposedly dead and gone person is trying to speak to us. We would also know to talk back. Most of us just brush aside gentle attempts at communication as imaginary, and thus meaningless, or as the effects of lingering grief. The souls trying to break through become annoyed after being ignored. Sometimes they become angry or hostile. Their efforts to elicit attention then take a decidedly more forceful turn. They are desperate to be recognized and addressed.

Such was certainly the case with Rebecca. The rare blood type she found on her sheets had no significance to her until she found out that her grandmother, who had passed on some years earlier, had had that blood type. Sure enough, during the afterlife healing circle Jana conducted, Rebecca's grandmother came forward eagerly, just bursting with things she wanted to tell Rebecca. Afterward there were no more blood-stained sheets.

The demise of the physical body does not of itself endow a soul with wisdom or ultimate enlightenment. This assertion contravenes extremely ancient and well-entrenched beliefs about life after death that are rooted in many different religious traditions. All of them in their own way state or imply that we attain some sort of improved or possibly perfected state after death, on the condition that we have been good enough, however that particular doctrine defines "good." This belief is also present in academia. Laura Markwick Kirkby's thesis from Chapter 2 stated, "...anything alive is progressively dying. From this perspective death ends the physical dying process and hence can be considered to be a healed state."[3] But as you recall from the previous chapter (please re-read it if not), souls not in a physical body were hardly healed or enlightened or all-knowing, all-wise. They had issues with those still in body and sometimes expressed their frustration in inappropriate ways, such as continually pestering their parents-to-be, just as children in physical bodies do.

"When you die, you don't become immediately self-actualized," said Julie Beischel, PhD, director of The Windbridge Institute. She was talking with Angela Artemis, the host of the *Powered By Intuition* online podcast. She continued, "I was surprised to learn that dead people are not scary, because popular culture will lead you to believe they are. They are just people with no bodies."[4] Julie, who earned her doctorate in pharmacology and toxicology, has learned about the dead through her extensive experiences putting mediums communicating with disincarnate souls through rigorous scientific testing of their accuracy.

The stereotype she talks about still prevails, alas. Many people who don't consider themselves formally religious are still secretly convinced that a nonphysical being is bound to be enlightened and wise. This is why many such people give undue credence to messages from mediums in a trance state. This stereotype is also why so many people conduct their own impromptu séances, hoping to contact some disincarnate guru or master. They'll contact someone, all right. It's really very easy to communicate with discarnate beings. The problem isn't departed loved ones with whom we share an emotional bond. The problem arises when cosmic curiosity-seekers make casual contact with a disincarnate jerk that plays mind games. Or, far worse, they tangle with a denial spirit. Or they inadvertently tune into a soul that would be labeled crazy if it were still dwelling in a physical body. For example, if a person in a mental institution dies while sincerely believing that he is Jesus Christ, his belief is not going to change merely because the physical body has ceased. Although no longer in a physical body, that soul will still believe it is Jesus Christ. And it will be more than happy to convey the words of "Christ" to anyone willing to pay attention.

Consider this from another perspective. Most of us would never open the front door to our homes and yell, "Come on in!" to anyone passing by. Most of us also would not regard a solo walk at 3 a.m. through New York City's Central Park as a very prudent thing to do. Yet people who misuse the séance for casual spiritual voyeurism are doing the equivalent of inviting strangers into their homes and lives or walking alone in the park after dark.

Are we saying that all messages from psychics or mediums are from deluded or mentally ill souls or worse? No. Mediums and psychics are often helpful, especially when we are having problems trusting or understanding messages from the dead or the not-yet born. These difficulties happen all the time because most of us have been taught not to believe or even acknowledge the very spiritual abilities that enable us to communicate with the other side, with soul-energy.

Let us now review these abilities and their many uses, including in the afterlife healing circle.

Chapter 8

One of the central tensions of modern living is a widespread sense of disconnection from the spiritual coupled with an almost equally ubiquitous longing to reunite with it. From the number of books about children and near-death experiences or children and past-life memories, there also seems to be a pervasive belief that newborns and children are somehow closer to the other side.

But no matter how old we are, we are still connected to the other side, to heaven, or to whatever name we have for it. *We simply do not recognize that connection for what it is.* To a certain extent, this perception of separation arises out of the conditioning and programming we receive as children from our families and society that emphasizes the concrete, the material, and logic at the expense of the imagination, the non-material, and feeling—the non-rational. Conditioning and programming are two of the reasons we often struggle to know the spiritual and emotional parts of our being through what seems to be a fog or veil.

Another major factor in the separation between this side and the other side is the harmful effects of non-vibrating self-judgment on the vibrating fields of human consciousness. What do we mean by this? Remember, consciousness and energy are equivalents (Chapter 7), and they vibrate, but self-judgment does not vibrate. It's beyond the scope of this book to explain exactly how self-judgment impairs and hamstrings consciousness, but suffice it to say that we are strangers to our deeper selves and to our innate connection to spirit as created souls (the other side) precisely because we suffer from the pernicious effects of self-judgment.[1]

If we are to succeed with the afterlife healing circle as we practice it, we *will* contact the other side, the world of spirit. This means we need ways to interact beyond the five physical senses of sight, sound, taste, touch, and smell. Like so many of us, John L. Johnsen, an independent producer based in Florida, talks about these non-physical channels of communication as a "sixth sense," but we actually have a sixth, seventh, eighth, and ninth sense, known collectively as psychic, or *psi*, abilities. Other names for these senses are intuition, instinct, hunches, or gut feelings. So instead of a "sixth sense," we call them "soul senses" because they are some of the abilities of the spiritual body, or unconscious mind. The soul senses truly are some of the gifts of the spirit mentioned throughout the Bible.

The soul senses are also the primary means by which we are able to apply the principles of love, connection, and trust. We need the soul senses to invoke and feel the presence of love-energy. We also require these non-physical senses to detect the presence of the soul(s) to whom we wish to speak, as that consciousness does not come attached to a physical body. We also need to learn to trust the information we receive through our soul senses no matter how illogical or strange it may seem.

These are the challenges inherent in our version of the afterlife healing circle, but they are not all that different from the challenges of any kind of spiritual activity. How much do we trust what we receive? Do we pay attention to it and act on it? The afterlife healing circle is a good way to engage consciously with our spiritual and emotional natures and strengthen our trust in this half of self.

In brief, the four soul senses are:

1. Soul vision, also called clairvoyance
2. Soul understanding, also called clairaudience
3. Soul feeling, also called clairsentience

4. Soul awareness, usually included with clairsentience but actually its own distinct channel of communication

There may be additional channels of nonphysical communication, but these are the ones we know and use every day.

Paranormal researchers often refer to psi abilities as *telepathy*, *precognition*, *psychokinesis*, and *clairvoyance*. The first three names, however, more properly describe *what* is taking place instead of *how* the nonphysical, intuitive information is being transmitted. Some specifics will make this distinction clearer: Telepathy is mind-to-mind communication, and it can take the form of thoughts (soul awareness), visions (clairvoyance), feelings (clairsentience), or even an understanding or words heard inside the head (clairaudience). The same applies to precognition. It is possible to have a vision of a future event, or a feeling, or an understanding, or simply to know that an event may take place. We have mentioned psychokinesis before. It happens when energy interacts with matter, something we do every time we meditate or visualize to relax our muscles or lower our blood pressure.

The difference between the soul senses and their physical counterparts is intensity. The experience of the physical senses is far more forceful than the soul-sense counterpart. Material colors are more vibrant, material sounds are more elaborate, material smells are more distinct, material tastes are more complex, and material touch is stronger than the nonmaterial. This is one of the reasons souls return again and again to a material reality—to avail themselves of a far stronger, richer, more involved sensory experience.

Just as the five physical channels of communication bring us information in material form, the four nonphysical senses convey information that is in nonphysical, or spiritual, form. We may infer, then, that energy in any form, material or nonmaterial, is also information. When we use our soul senses, we are simply scanning and interpreting information as energy instead of as matter, for which we use our five physical senses.

We may also infer that the two sets of senses are interrelated, because we already know that matter and energy are one and the same, differentiated only by their varying ranges of frequencies. Think back to the turned-earth smell that helped alert Richard to the presence of his friend's dead father. The soul's intense desire to gain Richard's attention evoked the material sense of smell. In addition, when we use our soul senses, we are activating the subconscious mind, or emotional body, and the unconscious mind, or spiritual body. This is the half of self that is capable of connecting us with souls who do not have physical bodies. We cannot reach or interact with discarnate souls through our conscious, rational mind.

Although they may seem weird to the rational part of our mind, the soul senses really are not any more mystical or magical than the physical senses. As souls in physical bodies, almost all of us possess all four nonphysical channels of communication. Unfortunately, very often the information the soul senses bring to us cannot be quickly verified through one or more of our physical senses. And while we are in physical bodies, we tend to believe that the physical is somehow more real than the nonphysical. Yet our feelings, similar to odors in the air, are real enough, even though we cannot see or touch them.

Moreover, the conditioning and programming we receive from birth on teach us not to acknowledge and certainly not to trust the nonphysical senses, because they do not function in a rational manner. Of course the soul senses are not rational. They are not meant to be rational. They exist for a different purpose. We lop off fully half of our being, the emotional and the spiritual, and relegate this huge part of self to second-class status, when we ignore or deny the nonphysical information we receive constantly through our soul senses.

Small wonder the dead and the not-yet born seem so far away. We are socialized from birth to discount and distrust the very half of self that connects us to the other side.

Because the soul senses do not function the way the rational part of our mind does, it helps to describe how they operate, to make it easier to recognize their subtle signals.

- *Soul awareness* does precisely what its name implies. It arrives as an instantaneous aware-ness about some situation or person, even if we've only just met the person or encountered the circumstances. We know, but we can't explain why we know or how we became aware. And, frankly, we don't care how or why we know; we just *know*. Awareness works the fastest of all the soul senses and is the only soul sense that needs no interpretation at all. The information is plain.

🌀 *Soul feeling* manifests as physical sensations on or within the body and are especially strong in the area of the solar plexus, but can be located anywhere. What these physical sensations mean will differ for each person, which is why it is impossible to interpret them accurately for others. As we pay closer attention and our ability to detect soul feeling improves, we begin to take note of a particular sensation and what event or situation it preceded. In that way we build our own personal "feeling library" and never need to consult anyone else to obtain the meaning of our own, unique soul feelings.

🌀 *Soul vision* (literally) shows itself either as pictures inside the head or as a visualization that appears external to self. It is the best known of the four soul senses, although it takes longer to express than soul awareness or soul feeling. Soul vision can be symbolic, or it can unfold a very detailed view of events that either have already occurred or may happen, depending on the intents of those involved. Again, any symbols perceived through soul vision are unique to the person receiving them.

◎ *Soul understanding* seems like a plodding tortoise compared to the other three non-material channels of communication. Soul understanding is just that: it arrives as an understanding. Soul understanding also conveys words or phrases that are heard either inside the head or as spoken words.

Each of us possesses all four of these soul senses in greater or lesser degree. But just as we usually favor one hand or another, or have one eye or leg that's stronger than the other, each of us has two stronger soul senses and two weaker ones. Before birth, some of us will opt to be strongest in soul awareness, then feeling, then understanding, and vision last. Others will reverse the order. Still others have entirely different soul-sense strength orders. Each of these soul-sense orders conveys definite personality traits and gives us certain abilities and certain weaknesses. Those strongest in awareness, for example, are terrific at public speaking, because what they need to say flows quickly and naturally into their conscious minds. Those strongest in soul understanding are naturally disciplined. The reason we choose a specific strength order has a lot to do with both the lessons and purpose we choose for a physical lifetime. One way to be certain of the order we chose is to ask our spirit guides, or angels. (We will say more about their intimate role in the afterlife healing circle in the coming chapter.)

Keep in mind that no order is better than another. Some people are distressed because they find it difficult to see auras. This may merely mean that they are not strong in soul vision. However, they may be able to develop their feeling or awareness and read an aura just as precisely through the other soul senses. For example, soul feeling is how Jana detects auras, and her accuracy constantly amazes those whose auras she scans.

In the eastern half of the world, the majority of people are strongest in soul awareness and soul feeling, whereas people in the western part of the globe are just the opposite—predominantly strongest in soul vision and soul understanding. This is a big factor in why East and West are so very different and have such trouble relating to each other. But it also sets up more diversity in people's worldviews and perspectives, which can be advantageous, provided we know about the different soul-sense orders and respect the strengths and opportunities of each perceptive mode.

Most of us find that our two strongest soul senses are so intertwined with our physical senses that we just assume that how we perceive and process information is the way everyone else thinks and processes it, too. That is not so. It is important to become well-versed in the different modes of perception conveyed by our own and others' varying soul-sense strengths, so that we may learn to communicate respectfully with everyone.

Although our soul senses are usually "on" all the time, they fade into the distant background of our everyday lives because we are not paying attention, out of misunderstanding and that tragic lack of self-trust. We notice only when information comes through one of our weaker soul senses because we tend to notice such unaccustomed forms of perception. Think back to Jana hearing the voice of one of her spirit guides outside of her head. Yaqui was communicating through her absolute weakest soul sense, soul understanding. It commanded her attention. The same happened when Astrid heard the joke in the shower. Her father was reaching out through her weaker soul sense in order to break through to her.

This also plays out in Eastern mystical traditions, which place a high value on visions. Visual information stands out to those in the East precisely because the dominant soul senses in this half of the world are not visual. People who reside in this part of the globe tend to receive intuitive information through soul awareness and soul feeling, but these two communication channels seem so mundane that they do not give their feelings or awareness as much credence as they do their less frequent visions.

We have been discussing one of the big challenges to the success of the afterlife healing circle: participants' ability to believe the information they receive through their own soul senses. Most of us simply do not have much faith in intuitive or nonphysical information, provided we even recognize it for what it is in the first place. Nor do we have much trust in self. The two issues are actually related.

John, the film producer, often receives fleeting feelings that he instantly dismisses. "I'll note it at the very mildest levels and then just let it go," he said.

On occasion, John's intuition is a little harder to ignore. A couple of days before receiving word from his son about his daughter-in-law's pregnancy, he knew something was up and heard a little girl's voice inside his head saying, "Hi, Grandpa."

"I said to myself, 'Now that's just got to be strange,'" he recounted.

Before his daughter-in-law gave birth, John felt the soul's presence leave the tiny body. "She just wasn't there anymore," he said. The baby was born with a severe birth defect and lived only a few days.

Later John sensed that the soul had returned, and, sure enough, word came that his daughter-in-law was pregnant once again, giving birth this time to a healthy baby girl.

Many of us have to learn the hard way to start paying attention. "I learned a big lesson when I found out I was really pregnant, and now I take those feelings quite seriously," said Deborah, who dismissed intuitive messages from her fourth child that turned out to be accurate and valid.

Honoring our intuition is really about learning to trust ourselves, a huge issue for most of us. Lack of self-trust is why so many of us turn to the Ouija board or table tipping. Both function as physical props that we can latch onto when we are not able or willing to rely on our soul senses. The problem with these tools is that they put frustrating limits on the conversation either by confining the communication to *yes* and *no* (table tipping) or taking a long time to spell out even short answers (the Ouija board).

"A lot of questions are not yes-or-no," Michigan resident Deb Christiansen told us. She and about seven of her friends have been table tipping on a regular basis for several years. At first they relied exclusively on two taps for yes, and one for no. But soon that wasn't enough. Having become more adept and more confident, she said, information now will "pop into" their heads (soul awareness at work here), and the table's movement simply confirms it.

Conscious experience of our soul senses endows us with ownership of the information we receive. This makes an enormous difference and is part of the afterlife healing circle's real power to transform through being actively involved in communicating instead of just a bystander, such as when we have a medium or a psychic provide information for us.

"When you go and get a reading, you are just hearing words," said Rondi, the mother of the twins we met in Chapter 5. "It's an intellectual understanding, but you are not getting caught up emotionally. The healing circle was a total experience—mental, physical, emotional, and spiritual—that engaged us on every level."

Marc, her husband, added, "The healing circle is a lot different than any kind of reading I've ever had, and I've had a few dozen of them. It's very different to get into that vibration, especially due to the circle arrangement. Everybody was enabled. Everybody was filling in each other's blanks."

@ @ @

So just how do we attain this enabled state, even if we do not think of ourselves as psychics or mediums? How can we possibly fill in others' blanks intuitively?

It's truly not all that difficult, especially because we're doing it already. Don't think so? Ever had the phone ring and know who's on the other end of the line, even when that person hasn't called in a while and there was no reason to expect a call? Ever entered a seemingly empty room only to retreat quickly because it was so uncomfortable? Both are instances of soul senses providing nonphysical information.

The soul (or psychic) senses do not strike uncontrollably or randomly, as is commonly believed even by those who have done extensive research in parapsychology. It is more than possible to turn up the volume of these senses or turn them off altogether if we so desire. It is all a matter of paying attention and practicing. "Being psychic isn't so much a chance encounter with a fact of life unknown to me," Astrid explained. "It's much more a journey into the flow of energies that I focus my attention to."

Think of the soul senses as nonphysical energy-information receivers that work clearest and strongest while we are in receptive mode. This means we are open to our emotional and spiritual bodies and are calm and unpressured. This is the exact opposite of how our mental body takes in physical information. The mental body concentrates and pushes; the emotional and spiritual bodies relax and receive. We unlearn the way we have been taught to learn, because that approach does not work for the soul senses. So make a game of it in much the same manner as Deb and her friends do. The more joy and light we bring to exploring and using our soul senses in a directed and conscious manner, the easier it becomes.

Deep relaxation really aids the entire process. One great way to relax that we teach our students is blending the energy of our being—our thoughts and emotions—with the energies of the sky, a tree, or calm water. Blending energies is not at all about taking over or dominating. It is about simply becoming one with whatever we blend with. Blending is expanding our own separate soul energy into and with the sky, the tree, or the water. The energies are separate and distinct, and yet they meld together.

Begin by assuming a comfortable position and location, sitting or standing, as preferred. Feel the desire to blend in your heart. Do not rush this. Take the time to feel this desire as deeply and strongly as possible. Next, direct that desire down from the heart into the solar plexus, and from there outward and up into the sky, over to the tree, or down into the water.

Enjoy the expansive sensations that come from expanding the energy field. Take time to notice information that arrives about the sky, the tree, or the water. Expanding your energy field makes it far easier to pick up information about that with which you blend. Don't try to force any information, however, and don't try *not* to try. Just be receptive. Allow any information or perceptions to flow to you naturally.

Once you have become comfortable with blending into the sky, a tree, or water, and using that to help you relax, you may try blending with a person, using the same process as before. In blending energy with a person, you actually go into that person's own soul nature, and receive information back via your soul senses. The same blending process allows us to read accurately the energy of a particular group. You are literally expanding your individual energy-consciousness into the energy of a group consciousness. In so doing, you receive information that is specific to each unique group, and allow the members to hear what they as a group need most to hear.

Blending with a group is how the best charismatic talkers and speakers work. They not only blend their energy with other people, but they are also pulling or attracting the energy of each person in the group into their own. In doing so, they establish a rapport and command greater attention, because their audience can feel with them.

Those not well-endowed with soul feeling tend to find blending a bit of a mystery until they have practiced it a while and start to sort out all of the sensations that come their way when they are blended. Instead, they may enjoy blending with a photograph. It is relatively easy to intuit the energy of a person in a photograph, which is probably why many native peoples do not care to have their pictures taken.

For this exercise, you need one or more photos of someone you don't know but whom someone else present does. Blend with one of the photos. Have a pen and paper handy and write down every quality or character trait the photo reveals about the person in it. Check the accuracy of this information by discussing it with the person who knows the subject in the photo. The results may be astonishing.

There are plenty of resources on the Internet and in many other books if you want more information about developing the intuitive side of your being. Invariably, we find that when we get in touch with our soul senses and begin to use them consciously and with purpose and direction, we become much better acquainted with our deeper selves and become aware of a far larger reality.

The distance between us and the dead or the not-yet born, and the invisible helpers we have by our sides, shrinks considerably. The gap also closes between our painful loss of a loved one or our uncertainties about impending parenthood, and the resolution we need.

Now we are ready to talk more about the invisible helpers that keep the afterlife healing circle safe—provided we know to include them.

Chapter 9

Even though at times we may feel alienated, isolated, and bereft, none of us comes into this world entirely on our own. We always have help and friendship right by our sides in the form of loving, invisible mentors who want nothing more than to play an active role in supporting us before, during, and even after our physical sojourns on Earth. All we need do is ask for their help—and then be ready and open to receive their guidance. (The blending exercise from the previous chapter can help us open up.)

As vibrating, eternal soul-energy, we choose to experience each physical lifetime. We usually have a purpose for the life we have selected. Such purpose is general, such as teaching, healing, counseling, inspiring, creating, being of service, and so forth. Our life purpose immediately attracts to us other spirits who want to share that purpose but do not necessarily desire to do so in a physical body. We then select a group of souls to help us along the way. Often we make our choices based on the fact that we know these spirits already from other physical lifetimes on Earth (or elsewhere). We trust these beings and they trust us. Sometimes we include souls who have a particular expertise that we believe will be especially helpful to us, and sometimes we just want to try something new while on earth.

Then we arrive in our physical bodies. As very young children, we interact with our spirit friends as the invisible companions we play with and who comfort us. Well-meaning adults, however, admonish us that these friends are "not real." We start to distrust our soul senses, the means by which we communicate with our guides. Eventually we give up on our soul senses and our friends so that we may "grow up" and become "well-adjusted."

Our guides remain with us anyway, sending us their love and support, hoping to reconnect in a more direct manner. They fulfill different roles on our behalf. Yaqui is Jana's spiritual growth guide, the one who is most focused on her spiritual well-being. Candace's spiritual growth guide is a soul she calls Sun. When Yaqui helps Jana with her teaching, counseling, or therapy, the entire room fills with the softest, gentlest energy that melts all hearts. Sun is very loving, too, but his essence has a distinctly intellectual cast to it. Between them,

Jana-Yaqui and Candace-Sun, they appeal to and connect with a broad range of people.

Many guides take on the function of jokester. By linking the mental and emotional bodies, humor is the easiest and best way to tune into our own heart's wisdom. Helping us uncover and appreciate the hilarity and absurdity in life also aids in keeping our spiritual connection alive and healthy through reconnecting with the emotional body. Many of us have attended a solemn occasion only to find we are thinking an absurd thought or making an outrageous observation. This is very likely our jokester's doing.

Guides are also healers, teachers, legal experts, even business consultants! One of Jana's guides is a handyman who invariably astonishes his physical counterparts. They cannot understand why or how Jana (with his help) is able to tell them the actual mechanical problem even before they inspect the broken machine. This guide, who calls himself David, also examines every plane before Jana or Candace fly and sends back a report on its air-worthiness. We will not board any aircraft that does not meet with David's approval.

Guides usually reveal themselves to us in a form we can relate to, meaning human, but some guides have present themselves as comic book figures or cartoons—for example, Wonder Woman or Rocky and Bullwinkle—if that's what will help us bond with them. The forms and names they take on are simply a matter of making them, their love, and their assistance readily available to us by matching our needs and expectations.

Very often our guides know our deeper issues far better than we do at the conscious level. This makes them useful allies in bringing up children, particularly when they are very young. Many years ago, the 2-year-old granddaughter of one of our students started biting other toddlers at her daycare. The center threatened to expel the little girl, and her family was at a loss until her grandmother remembered to ask the child's guides for help. The woman reported that her granddaughter's guides not only explained the situation but provided successful suggestions for how to stop the biting.

Guides are also amazing when it comes to any kind of healing work. Jana and Candace tap the energy of their own guides and call on clients' guides when counseling and for sessions of Sunan therapy. When we cannot consciously fathom what the issue is or why we are acting or feeling a certain way, our guides help cut out the guesswork and can offer invaluable advice and options that are unique to each of us, our purpose, and our emotional and spiritual needs.

Is it possible for all of us to meet our guides, up close and personal? Of course—provided we are willing to trust our soul senses. Because guides do not have physical bodies (except in rare cases of extreme emergencies, when they can materialize[1]), we cannot sit down with them for a cup of coffee and a chat. We rely on intuition—our hunches, gut feelings, visions, and inner hearing—to be able to receive their messages and send ours in return. One way to reignite our relationship with our guides is an introductory meditation, which we can do on our own or with help if needed. However we choose to become reacquainted with our guides, the energy and effort we put into doing so will come back to us many times over in the form of increased feelings of love, acceptance, and well-being, not to mention all the practical help they will provide. Their (nonexistent) fees can't be beaten, either.

@ @ @

Although they are as loving and supportive as they can be, our guides want us to know that they are not perfect by any means. They are souls on their own journeys of spiritual growth and self-discovery, just as we are. We and they have simply agreed to travel together for a while to help each other. Yes—as imperfect and screwed up as many of us believe ourselves to be, we still have something to offer our guides. It takes regular and deliberate, conscious communication with them, however, to make the exchange a two-way street.

Our guides also want to emphasize that they cannot command us in any manner—how we feel, what we believe, or the actions we perform. They cannot violate our free will. They are mentors—trusted advisors—not dictators. We, the authors, are not the only ones sending this message. It comes also from observations by mainstream professionals such as psychiatrist Gerald Epstein, who noted in a book published many years ago that the "inner guides" who appeared to his clients during meditation would not act unless the clients specifically asked them to do so.[2]

Think back to Jana's first encounter with Yaqui. He encouraged her to frame her words as a request ("Are you asking?") so that he was free to start helping her in a direct manner. Jana also recalls being harangued one time by Manta, her healer, who may not have been the most enlightened soul to join a group of spirit guides. Manta was using a lot of "You should" and "You must" and being very forceful about telling her what he thought she was supposed to be doing. Suddenly, Manta's energy abruptly vanished and the lecture ceased. He returned a bit later a lot softer and less insistent. "As I was *suggesting*," he began again. Yaqui had taken Manta aside and reminded him about the limitations that free will places on guides' actions and behavior. Because Jana has been communicating directly with her guides for many years, she has provided Manta, Yaqui, and the others in her group with many opportunities for their own spiritual growth. They appreciate it deeply and return the favor every day.

The same principle that prevents guides from violating our free will, even to help us, also applies to souls not in body who try to communicate with us. If we consider these souls annoying or disturbing, we may tell them to cease and desist, and most of the time they will heed us. We'll address the issue of how to handle the ones that ignore our requests shortly.

Exercising her right not to be pestered is exactly what Rayni did. After two years, she'd had enough of being importuned by the soul trying to come in as her last child, so she told him where to go, so to speak. It worked. Candace also has had visions of a person trying to use energy to find out what was going on with her. Candace silently told her to back off, and she did. Candace also asked her guides to help keep her energy at bay.

One last point about free will and spirit guides. Because guides do not impose their mandates and values on us, they similarly fail as a credible crutch to shield ourselves from our true responsibility. Jana and Candace are always skeptical of phrases similar to, "My guides are telling me to do such and such," or the ever-present variant, "The universe is telling me...." We don't buy it. Guides and the universe (and even God) are not in the business of ordering our lives. That's our job. But our guides will help us explore all of our options, which our fears or other limitations often prevent us from perceiving.

In addition to emotional and spiritual support, guides act in two capacities directly related to what they do during the afterlife healing circle. We have already mentioned that guides are involved in all manner of healing. This includes energy-healing modalities such as Sunan therapy, and more conventional medicine, too. If guides will make their presence obvious in sessions between a psychiatrist and his patients, they'll participate in any kind of healing, provided they are invited to join.

The other related role for spirit guides is that of protector—probably their best-recognized function. In our world full of cars, buses, trains, planes, boats, and other forms of mechanized travel, protectors put in plenty of overtime paying attention when we are distracted. The real wonder is that we have as few accidents as we do, especially in this age of cell phone conversations or texting while driving, walking, or otherwise engaged in what become hazardous activities when we are not paying full attention. As psychiatrist M. Scott Peck concludes in his book *The Road Less Travelled*, each of us has protection all around us all of the time.[3]

It is critical that we make use of this protection at a certain point in the afterlife healing circle, as we will outline in the next chapter. When we do ask for their assistance, it does not matter whether or not we know the names of our guides. What does count is that we deliberately call on them for protection for each circle. They will be delighted to comply with our request.

Think of guides as spiritual bouncers, keeping at bay all manner of discarnate jerks and game-players and, even worse, attacks or attempts at possession. They reduce the incidence of weird or unsettling phenomena to pretty much zero, too. Jana and Candace have conducted and participated in many, many healing circles. With our guides' protection, we have never experienced any floating horns, disembodied voices, spooky mists, or any other odd events—with one exception...

We often use chairs that swivel because they make it easier for all those involved to reach a comfortable position in the circle arrangement. One time, before the start, one woman's chair kept moving slowly back and forth, even when she pulled her feet off the floor and no one else was touching the chair. The floor was reasonably level, and no one else's chair was moving unaided. We chuckled and went back to the task at hand. Once we called on the guides, the movement ceased.

That's the extent of the paranormal activity we observed during the afterlife healing circles we have been involved in. Of course, if that's what you're looking for, you can certainly find it, whether you use the afterlife healing circle approach or rely on the Ouija board or table-tipping: just omit asking for protection, and let the fun begin. Yes, we are being somewhat sarcastic here, because without protection, what may well happen will not be amusing at all. It will be scary at least, if not downright dangerous.

We are convinced that if more of us were in conscious and frequent communication with our guides, there would be a lot fewer instances of hauntings, diabolic home invasions, and even possession, all of which are far more common than the media or religious authorities care to admit. Free will is such that even denial spirits must obey if we are clear in our own hearts that we have the right to be free from attack, and then summon our own energy and the protection of our guides and insist that all unwelcome invaders clear out. If we want the aid of a priest or shaman, that is our right, too, but we have the tools to keep ourselves safe on our own terms, provided we know to ask and then act on that knowledge. We are not helpless in the face of dark forces.

What we are discussing here might be mistaken for what is sometimes referred to as spiritual warfare, a practice that invokes energies to drive out so-called demons or evil from a location or a person. Spiritual warfare is an oxymoron. Waging any kind of war, even at the energetic level, is not a spiritual endeavor. Those involved in this kind of activity are intruding where they have not been invited. It is one thing to use our own energy (and that of our guides) to clear out the spaces where we live and work. It is also one thing to use our own energy (and that of our guides) to fend off unwelcome visitors or attackers. But it's another thing entirely to declare that others' spaces or bodies are corrupted somehow and anoint ourselves as the cleansing agents. Twisting energy to invade or control is a gross violation of free will and as such entails very unpleasant consequences for those who do it.

Again, this is about using our energy where we have a right to put it and in a manner that does not violate others' boundaries (another term for free will). When we visualize or pray for peace or healing, we are not trying to force the issue. We are making a request at the energetic level. It's important to feel the difference between energy that supplicates lovingly and energy that does not ask before it barges in to take over. The latter energy is neither loving nor helpful.

While standing guard against any would-be energy-invaders during the afterlife healing circle, our guides also lend their energies (meaning, their love) to those in the physical group, making the circle all the more effective. Group energy is a potent magnifier, which is why Jesus told his followers, "For where two or three are gathered together in my name, there I am in the midst of them."[4]

Jesus was talking about how group energy is even more of an attractor than the energy of just one person or soul, and how the energy of the group draws his presence in spirit. This same dynamic operates during the afterlife healing circle, when the energies of those in physical bodies combine with the love-energies of all of their guides to attract the soul(s) in question. The presence of all this love also helps magnify the energy-information gleaned through the soul senses, making it possible even for those without a lot of practice using their intuition to obtain helpful information.

Now we come to the point of reviewing the remaining steps involved in conducting the afterlife healing circle. Although this approach is flexible and adaptable, there is a sequence that, if followed faithfully, will keep participants secure and help make the circle successful in bringing about the healing resolution the inquirer seeks.

Chapter 10

We have mentioned the inquirer before. The inquirer is someone who wants to communicate with a soul not in a physical body. If we have made known that we are willing to conduct the afterlife healing circle, and a possible inquirer contacts us, then it's up to us to establish whether the inquirer has a legitimate need.

This is the time for a conversation and some gentle questions. Inquirers are often very emotional and want to disclose all they know about the beloved departed. Do not allow this. Instead, at the outset, explain that in order for the afterlife healing circle to work, the inquirer must not divulge any details about the soul in question (the deceased person whom the inquirer wishes to contact). This respects the left brain's need for specific evidence, as we will explain shortly.

Questions that we do want to ask include:

1. What do you want to get out of the afterlife healing circle?

2. Did you have a personal relationship with the deceased?

3. Have you felt or sensed this person's presence around you?

4. Has this person been on your mind or in your thoughts a lot lately?

5. When did this person pass over?

Be sure to ask the last question because in instances of a very recent traumatic death or suicide, the afterlife healing circle may not be successful. The soul in question may be confused about crossing over or just in an unaware state and not ready to speak to anyone.

Listen carefully to the inquirer's replies, and trust your intuition, those always-active soul senses. The inquirer's answers will help determine if the person is a good candidate for the afterlife healing circle. In instances of contacting the not-yet born, the first question still applies: What does the inquirer hope to get out of the circle? Please do not use the afterlife healing circle to find objects, lost wills, or assets of any kind—especially of the illegal variety. Remember: just because someone has asked for the circle, that does not obligate us to conduct one for that person. Not only do we have the right to feel comfortable with the inquirer, but we fare best by establishing some sort of rapport to help ensure the success of the circle. Also, do not force the afterlife healing circle down the throat of a highly fearful person. It won't be all that helpful, because a frightened inquirer will be in a state of heavy denial, and that type of inquirer is not passive during the proceeding.

After you've vetted your inquirer, choose a place to conduct the circle. Whereas the stereotypical séance is held at night, in a small, closed room that has little or no light and plenty of dark corners (to hide the special-effects apparatus for the faked floating horns, the mist, and the disembodied moaning and groaning), in reality, it is possible to conduct the afterlife healing circle at high noon in the middle of a field—if that time and location will make the inquirer most comfortable. We generally use the living room of a house and set the time during the mid- to late afternoon. If the circle is meant as a soul rescue, it's helpful to conduct it in the place where the lost souls seem to congregate. Throughout the proceedings, we keep the curtains open; if the session is at night, the lights remain on. We are not out to scare up any nasty surprises.

We arrange enough chairs in a small circle to accommodate all participants. We also put a box of tissues on the floor in the middle of the circle. They are always in demand after (and often during) the circle to mop up those healing tears.

The person who issues instructions and keeps the afterlife healing circle on track is called the conductor.

The conductor invites the remaining participants. Allow the inquirer to bring a trusted friend or relative if he or she so desires. The best group size for the afterlife healing circle is between four and eight people total. Larger groups are somewhat unwieldy, and discourage participants from speaking out about the information they are receiving from the soul in question.

Participants do not need training in using the soul senses. In fact, we try to include people who've not received any type of instruction in using their soul senses because they bring fewer expectations to the circle and thus are often more open to what does come through. But we also do our best to pick those who are able and willing to follow the three principles of love, connection, and (self-) trust. The best candidates to participate are loving and open-minded. Don't make the session more difficult by using it to try to prove something to a friend or relative who thinks any interest in this stuff is grounds for an insanity plea. Skepticism is fine; denial, however, will hamper what we are trying to accomplish by blocking the love and therefore the information flow.

Getting back to the initial questions we do—and don't—ask of the inquirer, remember that the less information the conductor and other participants possess about the inquirer and soul in question, the better. This is why we do not allow possible inquirers to tell us anything about the person they wish to contact. This deliberate lack of advance information helps assure the inquirer that participants received their information only from the soul in question and not from some other source. This is critical to help that rational left brain begin to trust the information the circle participants are receiving. Say as little as possible about the inquirer and the soul when inviting the rest of the participants. Just tell them someone needs the afterlife healing circle. Also make sure all participants know and understand their role during the circle as we explain it in this chapter.

If the conductor thinks it will help participants relax, arrange to play recordings of baroque or classical music while everyone arrives and gathers for the event. Anything by Bach, or Pachelbel's "Canon in D" are good choices. The idea is to begin lifting the group's energy vibration frequency while reassuring any member(s) with the jitters. Absolutely no heavy metal, rap, or pop music; their vibrations would be counterproductive.

The inquirer always sits right across from the conductor in the circle. The conductor decides where everyone else will sit. Again, use those senses to obtain an overall impression of the different soul energies of the participants. Then try to alternate masculine and feminine energies. This doesn't mean always alternate men and women. Some males have a very gentle energy, whereas some women's energy is strong, more push than pull. The mix of the two helps balance the love-energy flow around the circle.

If the inquirer has brought a friend or relative, seat that person to the inquirer's immediate left. The reason for this placement has to do with the flow of love-energy. The left side of the body is the receiving side, and the right side sends energy. When participants send love from their hearts, it will flow down their right arms through their right palms into the left hand of the person to their right. Love-energy from participants flows counter-clockwise around the circle. If the inquirer's supporter is to the immediate left, then the supporter's love is what the inquirer will feel most strongly in the flow.

After seating participants, the conductor reminds them about the important part they play in the afterlife healing circle and the role of the inquirer (keep reading for more details). Once participants are clear about what they are to do during the proceedings, ask all in the circle to join hands. Tell them to place their right palm on top of the palm of the left hand of the person to their right. Again, this is to facilitate the counter-clockwise flow of love from the participants.

Make sure that they are comfortable, as they may spend up to an hour in this position. The conductor then directs all present to close their eyes and focus on their breathing. Adding some basic biofeedback techniques for slowing down the breathing rate is helpful here. It's an excellent way to calm everyone and clear their minds for what's next. Once participants are calmer and their minds are cleared, the conductor may offer a simple prayer of thanks. At this point, Jana uses her soul-feeling to assess the group, and in her prayer she speaks directly to any lingering uncertainties she senses in the circle members.

Next, the conductor further lifts the energy of the group by asking members to imagine standing in a column of white light. They may see this light, feel it, know that they are in it, or simply understand it, according to which soul sense is strongest for each person. Jana always asks the circle members to lift their minds, hearts, and souls to their creator—and to their invisible friends all around them. She gives them a few minutes to enjoy that feeling of connection.

Next, the conductor asks participants to send out love from their hearts, down their right arms, and toward the person on their right until the love flows all the way around the circle. The conductor also asks them to use their soul senses to visualize that love or feel its vibration, to be aware that it is there or simply to understand that it is present. It is this love, which is magnified considerably by group energy and which includes the special love of the inquirer, that draws the soul to the circle and helps keep it there.

This turbocharged love feels wonderful, and instantly soothes all those in the circle. Sometimes it is a little too effective, and many of them simply sit in contentment and feel little compulsion or need to speak up. They have a job to do, however. They have gathered to bring forth information and aid in resolution, and have specific tasks to accomplish, as we shall find in a bit.

Now is the time for the conductor to lead all participants in calling on those invisible mentors and friends, even if it seems silly or as though it will not make a difference. It will.

Always ask aloud for protection.

Whatever names we use for them, whether we call them guides or angels or something else entirely, is beside the point, so long as we call on them to protect us during the circle. Guides cannot act without specific permission every time we conduct the afterlife healing circle.

After the conductor asks for protection out loud, the conductor then directs each person in the circle to voice (speak out loud) a request for protection. The conductor next asks each participant's guides or guardian angels to stand just outside the circle and allow in only the soul(s) sought by the inquirer. They'll be delighted to do so.

This one simple but absolutely crucial step will make all the difference in the world. Our guides' protection eliminates spook jerks, disincarnate crazies, and even denial spirits (also known as demons or even Lucifer himself). They'll just have to get their jollies at someone else's expense. Meanwhile, we can go about our healing mission in peace and complete safety. Amen to that!

Once the requests for protection have been spoken and the love is flowing around the circle, the conductor asks the inquirer to speak the name of the soul in question. The inquirer verbalizes the soul's full name two times and a pet name or nickname the third time.

Sometimes, the soul hesitates to enter the circle because there are strangers present. If that's so, the conductor should ask the inquirer to repeat the same name sequence aloud once more.

Other times, the soul is so eager to enter it doesn't wait until the inquirer has finished speaking for the first time. Usually, the soul will pass into the circle over the inquirer's right shoulder, but occasionally the entry point is different. It doesn't really matter. And often the inquirer or other members of the circle can detect the soul's entry into the circle even without the welcome from the conductor.

Once the soul is in the circle, the conductor's job is to keep it there by sending even more love straight from the heart. Most souls realize they need to assure the inquirer of their true identity. They almost immediately begin sending highly personal and sometimes very specific information about themselves. If the soul in question doesn't know what to do at this point, the conductor and other participants may ask it for evidential material and explain that the inquirer needs this information.

How does the soul send information? How do participants ask it questions? Through those four soul senses, which not only receive, but also convey thought-energy that is then picked up as images, vibrations, words, or awareness by participants' own intuition. Here is where our society's general lack of trust can be an issue, but the group love-energy also enhances the energy-information so that it is a lot stronger and therefore easier to send and receive. Provided the conductor is comfortable and confident with the process, other participants can be less assured and still be very helpful.

The work of the other participants is to verbalize what is called evidential material or trivia. It is vitally important that the conductor emphasize to all involved (except the inquirer) that they are to speak aloud every single piece of information they receive without editing. Again, this is where our general inability to trust our soul senses can really hamstring our efforts, because it seems safer just to say nothing and let someone else do the talking.

However, as Deb, the woman with a group of table-tipping friends, points out, "If everybody sits in silence, then nothing ever happens." She is spot on. The very act of speaking out loud helps keep the energy moving around the circle and encourages the soul to provide additional specific details. Free and open expression is a spiritual right, along with free will. When they do speak up, time and again, participants have pulled information seemingly out of thin air about people or events that only the inquirer or the soul in question could have known.

Very often, evidential information arrives in the form of physical sensations that can be unsettling, especially in cases of violent death or death from an illness such as cancer of the throat or lungs. A throat or chest may feel tight, or one or more of the participants may develop a pain in the head or some other area of the body. If for no other reason than self-interest, participants should verbalize what they are receiving or they will keep on experiencing the discomfort or pain. Speaking up frees them from the sensation, provided it is not theirs.

Even with these instructions and reminders, participants often still hesitate to say anything out loud, which is counterproductive. Jana, for example, was taking part in the afterlife healing circle many years ago and could tell that the man sitting next to her kept receiving something but was holding it back. After this happened three times, she encouraged him to speak up.

"This is really silly," he replied hesitantly. "It just doesn't make any sense. I see a white picket fence, but it's not upright. It's standing on one end."

The inquirer gasped, "Now I know it's my son!"

Years earlier, as a boy, the inquirer's son had taken an old piece of picket fence, turned it so that the posts were horizontal and nailed it to a tree trunk so that his dog could climb up and join him in his tree house. It was something only he and his grieving parent, of all the participants in the afterlife healing circle, would have known.

During her session, Clara was finally convinced of her mother's presence when one of the participants talked about seeing a field of red poppies, waving in the wind. Then another person mentioned a cross, while Clara's daughter immediately said she saw a skull.

"I knew it was my mother then," Clara explained. "Red poppies were my mother's flower. She had them all over the house when I was growing up. And the Skull of Adam forms the base of the Russian Orthodox cross.

My daughter wouldn't know that. She was brought up Presbyterian."

The point? As we have said before, the information the soul is sending is for the inquirer, not the participants. That is why it often seems strange to participants, and they are tempted to shift into their left brains to analyze it. Don't do that. Instead, speak up. The conductor will have informed the inquirer before the session begins to respond to each piece of information verbalized in one of three ways: "Yes," "No," or "I don't know."

Sometimes the soul in question provides information that the inquirer isn't sure of or simply doesn't know but can check out later with family or friends. To head the next question off at the pass, yes, we can use the afterlife healing circle to conduct crime investigations. We need one of two things for the session to be fruitful: the first is the active participation of a person with close emotional ties to the being against whom the crime was committed; the second is a request for help from the police. We have not been involved with any type of police work because local authorities, shall we say, look askance at intuitive methods of detective work. We have no burning desire to persuade them otherwise because we don't need to prove ourselves to anyone.

After the inquirer has been assured he or she has contacted the right soul, he or she is emotionally ready to continue to the next stage of the afterlife healing circle. This second phase consists simply of giving the inquirer and the soul the chance to talk to each other, assisted by the other session participants.

What comes out as a result of these discussions is usually loving and comforting, but not always. In one instance, the afterlife healing circle revealed the existence of past sexual abuse of the soul by the soul's mother, who was also the mother of the inquirer. One of the participants became so indignant that she almost disrupted the circle entirely through her energy and her comments. Try not to judge the information that comes forth, because again, that will shut down the love-energy flow. Should issues arise that require follow-up, there is a different time for and way of addressing those concerns.

The second part of the afterlife healing circle is always very emotional, if for no other reason than the inquirer finally has some evidence that a loved one thought dead and lost forever is, in fact, still living, if not in a physical body, and very much found. Or the inquirer finally has contact with a soul of a child not yet born. The evidence of such communication is provided partly through the trivia, which are necessary to satisfy the left brain. The heart, however, is much more open to messages from the soul. As the second half progresses, inquirers often begin to pick up thoughts and especially feelings from the loved one in the circle on their own.

When speaking to a child not yet born, Jana at this point encourages the parents to introduce themselves and ask the soul why it chose them as parents. The parents should also want to know what they can do to help the child fulfill his or her purpose for this coming lifetime. This will make parenting so much easier once the child is in a physical body again. Jana also takes the chance to encourage the soul to be fully present during birth to make the process faster and less painful, and to let the mother know if the fetus experiences any problems during the pregnancy.

The joy of such a reunion or meeting is impossible to comprehend except through direct experience. Resolution replaces anguish. Parent meets child, and both become better prepared for the years ahead together. Tears flow freely from relief, not grief, or from the joy of anticipation. The healing spreads from the inquirer and the soul to every member of the circle.

Once the inquirer and the soul in question have exchanged what they needed to say, the conductor steps in to offer a brief prayer and thanks to the guides who have helped keep everyone safe. It need not be lengthy or formal, and those who participated may also express their gratitude out loud.

We maintain a long list of current and former students, clients, and friends who have volunteered eagerly to be part of the afterlife healing circle whenever we hold one. They come out of love and a desire to be of service to others and are not paid any money for their time. Instead, we offer them coffee, herbal tea, soft drinks, or cold water. The time before and after the circle gives them a chance to catch up with old friends, make new ones, and chat with people who don't think all this stuff is so weird after all.

Likewise, we do not charge inquirers for the afterlife healing circle, although we do charge to teach people how to conduct them. Let's face it—among the public, the séance has a worse reputation than used-car dealers or TV pitchmen. Some even erroneously regard the afterlife healing circle as a form of devil worship, which it most emphatically is not. We avoid this issue entirely simply by never charging for the afterlife healing circle and by encouraging those we train also to conduct them at no cost as a community service. This means that we have only a limited amount of time to devote to the afterlife healing circle, which is one reason we wrote this book. We are hoping it will help spread a practice that can result in so much good.

Remember, anyone can rig up a floating horn or an "ethereal" voice in the dark, but no one, however well-versed in deceptive practices, can fake the *feelings*—the profound and powerful sense of relief and release that surrounds and embraces the inquirer, the soul, and the other participants during the properly conducted afterlife healing circle. It is the kind of healing that transforms lives—on this and the other side—forever.

Chapter 11

The afterlife healing circle can transform lives by providing much-needed resolution, but it is by no means always a resounding success. Those who insist on *no mistakes whatsoever* most likely will not be satisfied with this method of contacting the other side. For example, Jana once conducted the afterlife healing circle for a woman who insisted that the soul in question recall an exact moment on one particular day during their relationship, and feel about it the very same way she did. The soul was confused and exasperated because the moment did not hold anything close to the significance for the soul as it obviously did for the inquirer.

The latter left disappointed, and the others in the group were frustrated that the inquirer kept validating the information they were bringing forth, yet still said it was "not enough" to satisfy her.

Expectations invariably limit our ability to be open and receptive in many profound ways, so it's important to approach the afterlife healing circle with as few expectations as possible. We truly never know what information we will receive or how we will receive it when we contact souls not in physical bodies.

In one of our afterlife healing circles that allowed parents to meet their child in the womb, the soul clearly presented a male image and energy and even asked for a boy's first and middle name, to which his soon-to-be parents agreed. Yet a sonogram some weeks later in the pregnancy revealed that the fetus was female. Confused and disconcerted, the mother called us, and Candace did some automatic writing with a soul who calls himself Dr. Sunan. This loving healer was a physician in his most recent physical lifetime and is one of the leaders of the Sunan Society. Dr. Sunan told Candace that the soul in the womb intended to come in as a little boy, but felt tremendous hostility to that prospect from the expectant father and decided that might not be such a good idea. Dr. Sunan also explained that gender is highly fluid and not determined until much later in a pregnancy than medical science currently understands. The soul thus had the opportunity to change genders and come in as a girl. Candace provided Dr. Sunan's account for the gender shift to the mother, who was satisfied with it and just as happy to have a girl.

The afterlife healing circle is by no means the only method of soul communication. There is the ancient Greek technique of mirror-gazing made popular through a bestselling book by Dr. Raymond Moody.[1] Another bestselling author, James Twyman, was conducting experiments a few years ago in using lucid dreaming for soul contact. Each of these approaches has its own strengths and weaknesses, and may better suit many of us than the afterlife healing circle. It's up to each of us to discover our preferred method, and it never hurts to explore until we find something that feels right and provides the healing and resolution we need.

Often our fears or lack of trust make it simply impossible for us to use the afterlife healing circle or any other means of soul contact, at least temporarily. That is when psychics or mediums can step in to assist us. Mark Ireland, ironically the son of a very famous medium in the mid-20th century, Richard Ireland, found mediums enormously helpful to him after the unexpected death of his younger son, Brandon. His first reading was from Allison DuBois before she became a household name through the television series *Medium*. Mark, an Arizona businessman who authored a book about his search to come to terms with his loss, says, "Mediumship readings, I found, if they're good ones, can be very therapeutic for parents or anyone who has lost a loved one, child or otherwise." He was quick to add, however, that it's not a good idea to rely on mediums or psychics to the point of using them as a crutch. "I think a person has to develop their own sense of spirituality and not become balled up in this shell of grief," he said.[2]

We agree wholeheartedly, and know that the experience of using our own soul senses to obtain information from souls not in physical bodies is one of the fastest and most direct ways to grow in our spirituality and self-trust, which are intimately linked. There is no substitute for direct personal experience, however helpful and accurate a psychic or medium might be at pinpointing and delivering details and facts about a departed loved one. Facts and details may (somewhat) satisfy or even astound the conscious mind, but not the heart and spirit, which have very different needs.

When we focus solely on this physical world, we limit ourselves to a material reality and to the physical senses. Materially focused, we may have some vague concept of spirituality or a creative force or energy, but regard it all as far outside of ourselves. God is impersonal and irrelevant to us in our everyday material existence.

Materially focused, we believe we are bodies that may or may not have a soul. That soul, if it exists, has no role in daily life. It leaves that physical body at its death and somehow merges with this separate being called God—*if* the physical being has been "good" during life. If not, some sort of punishment awaits.

Materially focused, we generally believe that we have only one shot at life and that if something cannot be seen, heard, smelled, touched, tasted, or measured in some way then that something does not exist. It is part of that unknown, and whatever is unknown simply does not exist in our thinking as material beings. Rarely do we allow ourselves to feel or even become aware of our emotions because, after all, emotions are frivolous and irrational, which is bad to the materially focused.

When we focus solely on the material, our spiritual aspect may or may not be demonstrated through belonging to an organized religion or sect. As a rule, when we are solely focused on physical reality, comes from our validation outside of self. In other words, we have no value except as we prove that value to others. We as materially focused beings measure our self-worth by how much we possess and how much power we exert in the surrounding world.

Physically oriented, we are caught up in expressing self primarily through the mental body (conscious mind) and the physical body. The mental body believes that we must push for things in life; that if it's easy, it's not worth it; and that life is very complex and complicated. Perception through the physical senses is limited to appearances, some surface verbal communication, and superficial emotional sensations. Perception limited only to the physical senses lacks the ability to penetrate into the depth of issues or relationships to perceive the whole.

When we are focused solely in the physical, we are constantly affected by our environment and the problems of others. We frequently feel empty—a fraud, perhaps, an empty shell expressing ourself in a lack of self-worth, confidence, and continuity, depending on external experiences both for pleasure and for pain. As physically focused beings, we are slaves to the whims of society's standards and expectations. We also depend on the stimuli of pain and pleasure to believe we are even alive.

When we expand our focus to include the emotional and spiritual, however, we recognize first that we are souls that, at this point, dwell in physical bodies. We understand that as created souls, we are eternal, that we have lived before and will always live. We recognize that there is no final compromise, no final solution. When we enlarge our focus, we are aware of the utter simplicity in the truth that we are eternal energy-essences that continue to grow in awareness and knowledge until finally we come to realize we are co-creators with God—always have been, and always will be. We know to the core of our beings that we never cease to exist or to create.

Spiritually focused, we discern the environment and relationships with other people through our soul perception as well as our physical senses. In consciously employing all of our (at least nine) senses, we bring a depth of perception, understanding, and wisdom to the surrounding world. As spiritually oriented beings, we regard this world as a schoolhouse, this lifetime as an opportunity for growth, love, and understanding. We know we can communicate with our own souls through the soul senses and also with God and loved ones not in physical bodies. We also know we are capable of consciously tapping into universal mind at will in order to grow, to understand self, and to understand self in relationship to the surrounding world.

As spiritually focused beings, we also know our purpose and direction in the course of this physical world. We are consciously aware of our oneness with the Source, with the One, and perceive the oneness of all as a bonded unity. Our fears of death and the unknown diminish because we can feel the reality that there is no such thing as oblivion, only transformation. We know also that consciousness goes with the soul, that our uniqueness is expressed daily through a physical body, and that we in the physical world are not separate from or lost to spiritual realities.

As we expand our focus to include the spiritual, we are better able to affirm physical life through joy and happiness, and no longer feel so much emptiness within. Instead, we experience a profound connection with self, with God, and with all around us, whether people, animals, entities, or other things that exist within the physical and nonphysical realms.

The afterlife healing circle is a unique way to bridge what may seem an impossible chasm and disconnect between the material and the spiritual. Yet the reality is far more hopeful and loving, and the afterlife healing circle provides personal experience of that hope and love. It's up to us to exercise our free will and open our minds and hearts to the seemingly implausible possibilities the healing circle affords us.

As our invisible mentors and friends often bid us, go now in peace and joy with all our love.

Appendix:
The Steps in Brief

BEFORE THE START

The conductor determines the inquirer's motive in asking for the afterlife healing circle. Make sure it is for healing resolution or to solve a genuine problem that cannot be handled in any other way.

The conductor does *not* ask for details about the soul in question, but does make sure there is an emotional connection between the inquirer and the soul. In soul rescues, make sure there is simply a legitimate connection between the inquirer and the soul(s) in question (for example, the soul is causing problems in the inquirer's home or place of business).

The conductor invites two to five participants and encourages the inquirer to bring a spouse, trusted relative, or friend(s).

The conductor asks other participants to arrive earlier than the inquirer and instructs them that they are to verbalize everything they receive intuitively, no matter how strange. The conductor may play classical or baroque music softly in the background to help relax participants and start raising the energy vibration level.

When the inquirer arrives, the conductor makes the introductions and spends a bit of time to ensure everyone is as comfortable as possible. The conductor shares with the group as few details as possible about the soul in question.

The conductor shuts off the music (if it's playing) and seats the group in a circle, with the inquirer opposite the conductor. Alternate people with strong energies and those with softer energies. Put the inquirer's companion or the person with the most loving energy to the inquirer's immediate left. Put the person with the strongest energy to the conductor's immediate left to act as a "battery" for the conductor to keep the energy moving. Place a box of tissues nearby.

The conductor instructs the inquirer to respond to the other participants in one of three ways: "Yes," "No," or "I don't know." Nothing else.

As the Circle Begins

The conductor tells the seated participants to join hands, each person's right hand covering the palm of the upturned left hand of the person to his or her right.

The conductor leads the group in a relaxation meditation, using his/her intuition to sense when participants are as calm and centered as they can be.

The conductor asks aloud for protection and asks everyone to verbalize his or her requests for protection.

The conductor instructs the inquirer to speak aloud the soul in question's full name twice and nickname once. This can be repeated if needed. In cases where parents have not yet chosen a child's name, simply ask the soul waiting to be born to this mother or parents to come into the circle.

During the Circle

Once the soul in question enters the circle, the conductor reassures the soul that the group has gathered to foster communication between the soul and the inquirer. Other participants may also welcome the soul.

The conductor keeps reminding participants to verbalize any information or impressions they are receiving.

The inquirer answers only "Yes," "No," or "I don't know." The inquirer listens carefully to all information and responds as truthfully as possible.

Participants other than the inquirer must verbalize everything they are receiving. If they feel physical sensations and do not speak, they will continue to feel these sensations. Speaking releases the energy.

The conductor continues to move love around the circle throughout the session.

Once the inquirer is satisfied that the soul the inquirer seeks is in the circle, the group pauses to give both sides time to say what they need to say to each other. The conductor and the other participants may assist here if the inquirer seems hesitant.

Once the inquirer and the soul in question have said what they needed to say, the conductor offers a prayer of thanks for the blessings of the healing. If the soul is a departed loved one or an entity that has decided to seek another mother, participants may encourage the soul to move toward the light so that it may continue its path.

After the Circle

Participants release each other's hands and open their eyes. The tissues will be needed and welcome at this point.

Before disbanding, the group needs a bit of time to discuss and review the experience. The inquirer may now respond more fully to the information the other participants received and explain its significance.

Keep in mind that the afterlife healing circle is free-flowing, and each circle is unique in how it unfolds. As long as participants remember to ask aloud for protection, they can skip or forget every other step and still do just fine.

Notes

Chapter 1

1. Wagner, Stephen. "Terrifying Séances." About.com: Paranormal Phenomena. *http://paranormal.about.com/od/lifeafterdeath/a/aa100508.htm*, accessed March 2015.

2. Yahoo.com Answers. *https://answers.yahoo.com/question/index?qid=20071111105754AA6nfWG*, 2007.

3. Brian Dunning, personal interview.

4. Phyllis Sloan, personal interiew.

5. Phyllis Sloan, personal interview.

6. Astrid Stromberg, personal interview.

7. "Healing messages: The potential therapeutic benefit of mediumship readings in the treatment of grief (Research Brief)." The Windbridge Institute (2012). *www.windbridge.org/papers/ResearchBrief_Grief.pdf*, accessed March 2015.

8. Briana Henderson Saussy, personal interview.

9. DeRohan, Ceanne, *Right Use of Will: Healing and Evolving the Emotional Body*, Santa Fe, N.M.: Four Winds Press, 1984, 1986.

Chapter 2

1. Kirkby (née Markwick), Laura, "Circles of healing around the world: An exploration of the association between spiritual healing and circles in art," pp. 315–316, PhD thesis, Townsville, Queensland, Australia: James Cook University, 2004. *http://eprints.jcu.edu.au/7964/*, accessed March 2015.

2. "Circles," Restorative Justice Online, *www.restorativejustice.org/university-classroom/01introduction/tutorial-introduction-to-restorative-justice/processes/circles*. Reprinted with permission from *www.restorativejustice.org* (c. 2001–2014, Prison Fellowship International Centre for Justice and Reconciliation).

3. Jones, Dan, "New Light on Stonehenge," *Smithsonian Magazine*, October, 2008, pp. 36–46.

4. Kirkby, "Circles of healing," p. 23.

5. "Circles," Restorative Justice Online.

6. Ibid.

7. Ibid.

8. "Truth and Reconciliation Commission (South Africa)," Wikipedia, *https://en.wikipedia.org/wiki/Truth_and_Reconciliation_Commission_(South_Africa)#Impact*, accessed March 2015.

9. "Circles," Restorative Justice Online.

10. Ibid.

11. Bolen, Jean Shinoda, MD, *The Millionth Circle—How to Change Ourselves and the World*, Berkeley, Calif.: Conari Press, 1999, p. 14.

CHAPTER 7

1. DeRohan, Ceanne, *Right Use of Will: Healing and Evolving the Emotional Body*, Santa Fe, N.M.: Four Winds Press, 1984, 1986, p. vii.

2. Talmadge, Candace L., and Simons, Jana L., *Hope Is in the Garden: Healing Resolution Through Unconditional Love*, Dallas: Sattva Institute, 1999, p. 83.

3. Kirkby (née Markwick), Laura, "Circles of healing around the world: An exploration

of the association between spiritual healing and circles in art," p. 23, PhD thesis,
Townsville, Queensland, Australia: James
Cook University, 2004. *http://eprints.jcu.edu.
au/7964/*, accessed March 2015.

4. Artemis, Angela, "Among Mediums—An
   Interview with Author Julie Beischel, PhD
   (& Giveaway!)," PoweredbyIntuition.com,
   April 21, 2013, *www.poweredbyintuition.
   com/2013/04/21/among-mediums-an-inter-
   view-with-author-julie-bieschel-phd-giveaway*,
   accessed April 2015.

CHAPTER 8

1. Talmadge, Candace L., and Simons, Jana L.,
   *Hope is in the Garden: Healing Resolution
   Through Unconditional Love*, Dallas: Sattva
   Institute, 1999, p. 87.

CHAPTER 9

1. Talmadge, Candace L., and Simons, Jana L.,
   *Hope is in the Garden: Healing Resolution
   Through Unconditional Love*, Dallas: Sattva
   Institute, 1999, pp.37–39.

2. Epstein, Gerald, MD, *Healing Visualizations:
   Creating Health Through Imagery*, New York:
   Bantam New Age, 1989, pp. 212–213.

3. Peck, M. Scott, MD, *The Road Less Travelled*, New York: Simon & Schuster, 1978, pp. 235–243.

4. The Holy Bible: King James Version, Matthew 18:20.

CHAPTER 11

1. Moody, Raymond A., Jr., MD, *Reunions: Visionary Encounters With Departed Loved Ones*, New York: Ivy Books, 1993.

2. Ireland, Mark, *Soul Shift: Finding Where the Dead Go*, Berkeley, Calif.: Frog Books, 2008.